TALKING FOOTBALL
(HALL OF FAMERS' REMEMBRANCES)
VOLUME 1

AUTHORS: DAVID SPADA & ELLIOTT HARRIS
EDITED BY MELINDA SPADA

I hope you enjoy reading this as much as I enjoyed conducting the interviews.

David Spada

TALKING FOOTBALL
(HALL OF FAMERS' REMEMBRANCES)
VOLUME 1

Copyright © 2015 by (David Spada & Elliott Harris)

All rights reserved. No part of this book may be reproduced or transmitted in any form or by any means without written permission from the authors.

ISBN 13:978-1511648806
ISBN-10:1511648805

Printed in USA

Table of Contents

About The Authors 1

Chapter 1 Charley Trippi… 2

Chapter 2 Art Donovan 8

Chapter 3 Chuck Bednarik..18

Chapter 4 Marv Levy 20

Chapter 5 Y.A. Tittle 34

Chapter 6 Gino Marchetti..44

Chapter 7 Jack Butler 56

Chapter 8 Hugh McElhenny......................................64

Chapter 9 Don Shula 74

Chapter 10 Doug Atkins...80

Chapter 11 Mike McCormack 86

Chapter 12 Frank Gifford 94

Chapter 13 Yale Lary...102

Chapter 14 Bob St. Clair..108

Chapter 15 Joe Schmidt 114

Chapter 16 Raymond Berry 120

Chapter 17 Forrest Gregg..136

Chapter 18 Lenny Moore 144

Chapter 19 Bart Starr...154

Chapter 20 Willie Davis 162

Chapter 21 Tommy McDonald................................168

Chapter 22 Sonny Jurgensen 172

Chapter 23 Sam Huff 180

Chapter 24 Don Maynard 190

Chapter 25 Bobby Mitchell.....................................202

Chapter 26 Len Dawson 212

Chapter 27 Paul Hornung 216

Chapter 28 Jim Taylor 226

Chapter 29 Jim Brown 234

ABOUT THE AUTHORS

David Spada is a successful attorney whose dream was to become a sports talk show host. Elliott Harris is a former Chicago Sun-Times Quick Hits columnist who has covered the world of sports for decades.

David and Elliott teamed up in 2011 to host the sports podcast "Sports & Torts" on talkzone.com. "Sports & Torts" was a finalist for Sports Podcast of the Year in 2013 by the website podcastawards.com. David and Elliott have interviewed over 180 Hall of Famers from the world of football, baseball, and basketball since 2011. They are pleased by share their interviews with 29 Football Hall Of Famers who talk about their careers in this book.

Chapter 1

Charley Trippi

> College:
> Georgia
>
> Career History:
> Chicago Cardinals (1947–1955)
>
> 1968 Inductee Pro Football Hall of Fame

College Choice
A Coca-Cola man was an alumnus of Georgia, and he played football there. He talked me into taking a trip to Georgia. When I did, I was impressed and I stayed. I was a halfback at Georgia when I played there. Winning a championship, that's the thing you play for. It's something you live with the rest of your life.

Bidding War For Services After College
Back then the leagues were bidding for talent. Even during the war, they had people coming around saying, "We'll give you a hundred dollars a month until you sign your contract and it won't count against your salary." I stayed away from that because I promised Charles Bidwill, the Owner of the Chicago Cardinals that I was going to sign with him regardless of what the other league offered me.

I went to New York and talked to Dan Topping and another gentleman. They made a good offer to me for both baseball and football. I signed with the Atlanta Crackers to play baseball and I got a better bonus. I got a $10,000 bonus to play in AA ball. I had a good year. I hit .336. Then they wanted to sell me to the Boston Red Sox after that. I made up my mind. I just couldn't compete in both sports. The wear and tear was so hard because you're active every day. You have to perform every day. It's tough when you have to perform every day.

Plus, I didn't have much of a family life. I was away from home four months a year back then. I decided I was going to throw in the towel on baseball and just concentrate on football with the Cardinals. I always had ambitions of playing big league baseball, but as it turned out, the money in football was so attractive that I decided I'd stay with football. The thing that escalated the price of football players was the formation of the American League back then. They were bidding for talent. Then, it got to be about money. As it turned out, it was in the best interests for the ballplayers back then.

Back in 1945, there were two leagues competing for talent, the American League and the National League. It put me in a good negotiating position. I ended up with the Chicago Cardinals. Back then, the National League was more established than the American League. Plus, Charles Bidwill was very generous with my contract. He gave me a four-year contract for $100,000, and I was perfectly happy with it.

When Mr. Bidwill drafted me, we sat down and in five minutes he said, "What do you want?" I said, "I want a four-year contract for a hundred thousand dollars."

He said, "You got it." I didn't even worry about the American League then. I was happy with what I received from the Cardinals, so I didn't give them an opportunity to beat the price I got with the Cardinals. You see, the American League was just beginning to get established. I wanted to be with a team that was well established and in the game to stay.

When I signed with the Cardinals, Mr. Bidwill said he had a green backfield, which was comprised of Paul Christman, Pat Harder, Elmer Angsman, and me. That was his greatest ambition—to have a green backfield. He had a vision, with the green backfield, that we were going to win the NFL Championship, which we did. Unfortunately, Mr. Bidwill never lived long enough to see his team win it.

1947 NFL Championship Game Against Eagles
I had a good day. We played on a frozen field. We played in tennis shoes. I had a 50 yard run from the line of scrimmage and I ran back a punt about 65 yards. I scored two touchdowns. I never anticipated playing in tennis shoes and I never anticipated scoring a touchdown with tennis shoes. It worked out pretty good. We got better traction with tennis shoes. We went out to warm up with football shoes and we couldn't stand up on the frozen turf.

It wasn't my idea. It was a necessity. We couldn't stand up with cleats. We took them off as soon as we got on the field. We stood up and then we're falling down. We always had tennis shoes in our bags so we all resorted to tennis shoes to play.

Playing Multiple Positions
I started playing in high school, where I did everything. I played defense. We had the single wing back then. I was a tailback, I threw passes, and I punted. It just came natural to me so it continued on into college and then into professional football. To me it was just another thing really.

1948 NFL Championship Game Against Eagles
We won our division and played in the Championship again against the Eagles in Philadelphia. The night before the game we had a big snowstorm. The ballplayers had to get the tarp off the field. As we got the tarp off the field the snow kept coming down. We had a hard time trying to play a football game under those conditions.

Greatest Thrill In Football
Well the greatest thrill I ever got out of football was playing in the Rose Bowl. I played in the Rose Bowl in January of 1943. I got to play 59 minutes. It so happened we had a football player by the name of Frank Sinkwich, who was a real good football player. We had a scrimmage out there before the game. He got hurt. He couldn't play. During the course of the game we brought the ball down to the one-yard line. We called a timeout so Sinkwich could come in and score. He scored with a bad ankle. We allowed him to finish his career on top of the ledger.

Chicago Cardinals vs. Chicago Bears Rivalry

Anytime you have two teams in the same city there's a big rivalry. We had some tough games with them. They were a good football team. I can't remember ever losing to the Bears. The Bears built up a lot of football traditions over the years. They've had great football teams. Of course the people of Chicago recognize the Bears as the number one football team in the city. As it turns out, we were pretty competitive. Every time we played the Bears we did pretty good against them. I think the league put pressure on the Cardinals to move. They didn't want two teams in the same city. I think they bought out the territory from the Cardinals so the Cardinals could move to St. Louis. There was some money exchanged between the league and the Cardinals back then.

Chicago Cardinals coach Jimmy Conzelman grabs the hair of running backs Charley Trippi, right, and Elmer Angsman as assistant coach Phil Handler, left, grins after the December 28, 1947 National Football League Championship game.
Photograph copyright Associated Press

Chapter 2

Art Donovan

> College:
> Boston College
>
> Career History:
> Baltimore Colts (1950)
> New York Yanks (1951)
> Dallas Texans (1952)
> Baltimore Colts (1953-1961)
>
> 1968 Inductee Pro Football Hall of Fame

Notre Dame
You know, it's a funny thing. When I was at Notre Dame, I was better than maybe half the tackles there. When the war was over, I met a coach from Notre Dame in California, and he asked if I was coming back to school. I explained that I wanted to, but Frank Leahy had his pets and I wasn't one of them.

I had a fight with one of his pets. A tackle was holding me and I kept saying, "Hey, don't hold me, okay? If you can't block me, don't hold me." He did it a couple more times. Finally, I got sick and tired of it and gave him a couple of punches. Then we got into a real fight. Leahy came over and told us to shake hands. I said, "I'm not going to shake hands. He doesn't like me and I certainly don't like him." That was it. I think that was my ticket out of Notre Dame.

My mother was in shock, but I'll tell you the truth, I really wanted to go to Fordham. It was a ten-minute walk from my house and I was always a Fordham fan. In fact, I use to watch them practice in the afternoon. The coaches and priests used to let us watch practice. I was just happy.

So after the war. I saw the Fordham Athletic Director and he said, "Look, we're disbanding intercollegiate football, so if I were you, I'd go to Boston College." Then, I made up my mind, and went to Boston College.

Draft
We had guys come in who were first round draft picks and not know what football was all about. We had a guy we took in the 19th round, Raymond Berry, and look how he turned out.

You don't know about a football player till they get on the field. Believe me. The Giants drafted me, but I wanted to stay in college for two more years. I hoped after that, if I was lucky, somebody would draft me. That's why the Colts drafted me in 1950. On Sunday morning I'm leaving the Bronx to come down to Western Maryland to go to Colts training camp. I came out of church which was right across the street from where I lived. My father sees my car packed with my two pair of pants and about four changes of underwear. He said, "Where are you going?" "I'm going to Baltimore." "What are you going to do in Baltimore?" I said, "I'm going to try out for the football team." My father said, "Are you crazy?" Then, he hollered up to my mother, "Mary, those big guys will kill him down there!" He was wrong. I'm still alive.

Eating
They used to say, "Hey, run around, Donovan. You're killing the grass." If I told you the truth, I never worked out in the off-season. I never ran. I never did anything. The first day of fall practice was the first time I ran around a field, because I figured I had to conserve my energy.

A friend of mine called me and said, "Hey, when you die I'm coming up there to the funeral and I'm going to give the undertaker $1,500 to cut your stomach open and see all the junk in there."

I think in 13 years I did 13 pushups. I was told when I was playing by a member of the team I had to start working out better.

I said, "Do you want a defensive tackle or do you want a gymnast." He said, "Alright, don't worry about the pushups."

There was nobody who could beat me eating hot dogs. I loved hot dogs. I went home one time and on my way back, I went through the Holland Tunnel. There was a guy selling hot dogs on the roof of a real fancy truck. I ate so many that I ran out of money and I had to stop eating them. The next time I found the guy and stopped for some hot dogs, was about four months later. He told me he didn't know who I was or where I came from, but he really missed me. I was the best customer he ever had.

We had a lot of great times, a lot of great stories. These guys today just don't have the fun we had. I think it was the greatest time in football history because the guys grew old nicely and we just had more fun, seriously.

Don Joyce and Gino Marchetti had a chicken eating contest at training camp. I bet on Joyce and somebody bet on Marchetti. There were four of us betting and we bet a $100 a piece. It was a Sunday afternoon, and we ate a typical Southern Maryland meal; chicken, mashed potatoes and peas. Gino starts eating the chicken, but Joyce, he's eating the chicken, the mashed potatoes and the peas.

I said, "For crying out loud, Joyce, don't worry about the God damn potatoes and the peas. Eat the chicken."

Marchetti gets to about, I guess, 18 pieces of chicken, and I said, "Joyce, one more and we win." He says, "I'm still hungry."
He ate, I think, 26 pieces of chicken.

We didn't care if he blew up or not. We won the bet. He reached into his pocket and picks out three pieces of Saccharin and dropped it in his iced tea. He was watching his weight.

For four months in 2012, I didn't have one beer. I had a bladder infection. I was told I had cancer in my bowel so I couldn't have beer. I had to give up the Schlitz and the hot dogs. The only Schlitz I had in four months was the one I had with the doctor in the hospital. His boss caught us and he nearly got fired.

Early Colts Teams
We knew we were getting better before Johnny Unitas came. We had a couple of quarterbacks who were real good. One time we played Green Bay and they were pretty good, but we beat them.

We got on the bus up in Green Bay and Gino Marchetti says to me, "Hey, fatso, how good do you think we are?"

I said, "Gino, I think this is the beginning of a good football team. It certainly was since we had Weeb Ewbank."

Gino said, "He's a weasel, but he's a good coach." And that was it.

Playing The Chicago Bears At Wrigley Field
It was fun playing at Wrigley Field, and it was fun playing against the best. They had that old time band out in center field. They used to play a lot of marching songs, and we would march onto the field. We'd make like we were marching with their music. We all got a great kick out of that.

Les Richter
We were playing the Rams out in the LA Coliseum in 1954. Les Richter was supposed to be a tough guy and now we're playing him out there and Don Joyce is our kickoff man. He kicks the ball and the next thing you know we're running out to get onto the field. Joyce is standing in the middle of the LA Coliseum and Richter is lying down on the ground.

Joyce has got Richter's helmet in his hand. I said "What the hell did you do now, Joyce?" He says, "I was only protecting him."

He claims that Richter kneed him. He ripped Richter's helmet off and hit him in the face with his own helmet. I swear to God. We're standing there looking, and Richter's got his hands over his face, blood coming out through his fingers. They almost threw Joyce out of the League.

Bobby Layne
He was a hell of a football player and he was a real character. We're playing him here in Baltimore and we were putting a lot of pressure on him. We had heard about his shenanigans and everything. In the third quarter we rushed him and three of us were lying on top of him. He's

screaming and hollering and I said, "God damn, Bobby, you're breath! You must've had a hell of a night last night."

He looked at us and said, "Hey, I had a few at halftime."

Lenny Moore
The best football player I ever saw on the field was my teammate, Lenny Moore. He could do anything. He could've been an All-Pro defensive back. The guy was amazing, absolutely amazing.

1958 NFL Championship Game At Yankee Stadium
I got a great kick out of it because I lived 4 miles from the stadium and when I got introduced, everybody, including all my neighbors booed me. It was a great day, great day.

You know what, if you really want to know the total truth, we didn't know what the hell was going on. We didn't know there was overtime or anything else.

When we tied the score, I said, "What are we doing next?" The official had to tell us. I think he had to tell, Weeb Ewbank, our Coach, what was going to happen after that. I thought we were so much better than the Giants and I think we were.

I said to Gino Marchetti when the Giants went ahead, "Hey, Gino, if we lose this God damn game, it will be the greatest tragedy because we're so much better than these guys." He said, "You know, Fatso, you're right."

We got lucky and won.

Frank Gifford did not make a first down on two occasions. The first time Marchetti and I made the tackle. Big Daddy dropped over and he broke Gino Marchetti's leg. The second time was in the overtime. Gino wasn't even in the game. He was sitting under the goal post watching. The fellow who came and stopped Frank was Ordell Braase from South Dakota. He was another fine football player. He grabbed Frank Gifford and stopped him.

Frank was screaming, "I made that. I made that!"

I said, "Hey, Frank. You didn't make it. Why don't you stop the bullshit?" And that was it. He and I have been friends ever since.

Joe Schmidt

I was happy I played with a great football team with a great bunch of guys. I think the greatest thing that I ever heard a guy say about the Baltimore Colts was from a great linebacker from Detroit, Joe Schmidt.

He said to me, "You know what? I wish I had played with you guys. You guys really had a lot of fun and you were good." He's another great friend of mine. I made a lot of great friends playing.

Johnny Carson

Mr. Carson was something else. He was a real gentleman. In fact, I was on his show a couple of times. The first time, I was sitting in a room thinking, "What the hell am I going to do here all by myself and nobody to talk to?"

Then a guy knocks on the door and says, "Listen, the people alongside of you, they don't have enough room in their room. Can I open the door and let them in? They're going to be on the show." I said, "Sure, go ahead."

He didn't tell me it was a lady from the San Diego Zoo with all these God damn animals. I opened the door and here comes snakes and other animals. I'm from the Bronx. I don't know anything about animals.

The second best thing was Johnny Carson's band. Doc Severinsen and the whole band congratulated me and Doc said, "You should be on at least once a week."

Cooking with Julia Child

I didn't know who Julia Child was and I said, "Where are you from, Ms. Child?" I thought the way she talked she was from England.

She said, "Cambridge." I said, "Cambridge, England?" She said, "No, Cambridge, Massachusetts." I told her I went to Boston College and I used to go over to the square there and drink beer in Cambridge. She said to me, "I don't drink beer." I said, "You're missing something."

She was a nice lady, and to tell you the truth, we got drunk. It was on The Letterman Show and David Letterman also got drunk. We were drinking cognac and at the end of the show, the three of us went in the back of a small convertible and I couldn't get out. So, they had to stop and get her out first.

I said to her, "We'll stay here all night. I don't care. I laughed my rear end off. It was fun."

Walter Cronkite
I was sitting in a room before I went on with Johnny Carson and a guy says to me, "Hey, there's a man out here and he wants to meet you." I went out and it was the great TV announcer, Walter Cronkite. He was a war correspondent.

I said to him, "You wanted to meet me?" I couldn't believe it. He said to me, "Young man, don't ever change. Just tell the truth and you'll be okay."

To me, that was the nicest thing that anybody ever said to me. I couldn't get over it. Walter Cronkite, saying to me, a defensive tackle, that he enjoyed me.

I said, "Mr. Cronkite, thank you very much. That's the best thing anybody every said to me."

Book "Fatso"
My wife is the one that wanted me to write a book, not me. Listen, I'll tell you the God's honest truth. I'm an Irish Catholic, and the only book I have ever read in my life was the Catechism going to Catholic school. I'm telling you the God's honest truth.

What can I say? I just was lucky to play with great football players and I had Coach Weeb. The guys who played alongside of me, Marchetti, Don Joyce, Ray Krouse were just fine football players.

<u>Don Shula</u>
Don Shula, another teammate, and I bought a house and we lived together. Shula then was as wild as we were. I'm serious. We'd get in the house and we'd wrestle, those two guys against me. They'd get me down, and start walloping my ass and I'd be laughing so hard, I couldn't do anything. They just beat the hell out of me, but I loved it.

Photograph copyright Associated Press

Chapter 3

Chuck Bednarik

> College:
> Pennsylvania
>
> Career History:
> Philadelphia Eagles (1949-1962)
>
> 1967 Inductee Pro Football Hall of Fame

First Contract
I got a $3,000 bonus, and a $7,000 contract, which totaled out to $10,000. In those days, that was pretty good money.

Nickname
After practice, I used to sell concrete. That's where I got the nickname, 'Concrete Charlie'.

Background
My parents came from Czechoslovakia, and I was born into poverty, in Bethlehem, Pennsylvania. My life was tough. I started playing football at Bethlehem High School. In those days we played both ways. That's the way football was in those days. Today it's pussycat football.

Fingers
I've got crooked fingers. When I shake the hand of a little kid I'll say squeeze it, and I go "Oink, oink." The finger on my right hand is wired and it goes way out there. The kids say, "Oh," and run away.

Philadelphia Eagle Chuck Bednarik after his famous hit on New York Giant Frank Gifford on November 20, 1960. Photograph copyright Associated Press

Chapter 4

Marv Levy

> College:
> Coe; Harvard
>
> Organizations:
> Buffalo Bills General Manager (2006-2007)
> Coach
> 1969 Philadelphia Eagles (Kicking)
> 1970 Los Angeles Rams (Special Teams)
> 1971-1972 Washington Redskins (Special Teams)
> 1973-1977 Montreal Alouettes (Head Coach)
> 1978-1982 Kansas City Chiefs (Head Coach)
> 1984 Chicago Blitz (Head Coach)
> 1986-1997 Buffalo Bills (Head Coach)
>
> 2001 Inductee Pro Football Hall of Fame

<u>Early Years In Coaching</u>
I graduated high school during World War II. Twenty-one of my classmates and I enlisted in the Army Air Corps. Three years later when the war was over, I returned home. Then, I was recruited to play football at the University of Wyoming. I went to Wyoming, but at that time, they didn't give you a minute to study. There wasn't a free moment, and I was feeling bad about it. I had a high school teammate, Dudley Simpson, a highly decorated Marine during World War II, who was at Coe. At that point of time I had never heard of Coe.

Dudley said, "Marv come here. You can participate in sports and get a great education." I did, and he was right. I entered undergraduate school with the idea of going to law school. I was a very dedicated student, and I got good grades. School was important to me. I enrolled in Harvard Law School. When I left college my football coach at Coe, Dick Clausen, called me aside and said, "Marv if you ever want to coach, you've got a job here."

I entered law school, but about three weeks into it, I realized my heart was out on the athletic field. They allowed me to transfer to the graduate school of arts and sciences, and I got a Masters degree. Then I went to a prep school in St. Louis for a couple of years to teach and coach. While at the prep school there was an opening at Coe and Dick Clausen hired me. I was back there coaching football. I haven't regretted the change for a moment.

I was in graduate school at Harvard University and the headmaster was a man named Robert Cunningham. I still remember him and revere him as a great educator. He was looking for a teacher of English and History. He liked my credentials and called me in.

I said, "Mr. Cunningham, I'd love to teach, but I also want to be a coach." He said, "You can be the head basketball coach and assistant football coach." I took the job.

My wife-to-be asked how much they were going to pay me and I said, "I never asked him that." I took a job at Country Day, and was there for a couple of years before going back to Coe.

We had very successful seasons at Coe. Actually, Dick Clausen was picked as the Division III College Football Coach Of the Year. I think we were undefeated two years in a row. He went to New Mexico as head coach and I went along as a member of his staff. Two years later, Dick left to become athletic director at the University of Arizona, and they promoted me to head coach. At that time, I was the youngest major college head coach in the country. Forty some years later, I was tied with George Halas for the oldest coach in the history of the NFL. Don't question my durability. You can question some of my coaching decisions, but my durability is there.

Why I Went Into Coaching
I loved coaching. I loved the game. I loved the competition. I liked the camaraderie. I liked the excitement. I've said many times, as a coach you put in long, long hours. Certainly we did, seven days a week during the season for seven months, but I never worked a day in my life. It was pure joy and it just appealed to me. My father had been an outstanding athlete, too. I think he was named the outstanding prep basketball player in the city of Chicago back in 1915 and 1916. He encouraged me in sports.

When I was coaching in the NFL, I'd get letters from young guys who were going into the coaching field asking me to tell them how to become a NFL coach. I told them if that's the only way you're going to be happy, you don't want to be a coach. The odds are long that you will be fortunate enough to move there. Do the greatest job you can. I've known some coaches who coached for 45 years at one high school and just adored it, loved it, and are renowned for the job they did. You should coach because you love coaching, not just because you want to coach in the NFL. That won't occur in many cases.

Assistant Coaches Hired
I'm going to do some bragging now. After New Mexico, we had a couple of very good seasons. I was called to the University of California. I took over the head coaching job during a time of tremendous student unrest. There were no affirmative action program. We had to struggle.

I hired a coach out of high school, Bill Walsh. I hired a guy that was an intern at Cal at the time, Mike White, who later went on to coach in the pros and at the University of Illinois. I hired Bobby Ross, who went into the pros. I'm bragging now because thats some pretty darn good coaches. Dick Stanfel, who later became a tremendous line coach for the world champion Chicago Bears, was a member of my staff at Cal. I was one step away from hiring Dick Vermeil out of high school, when we all got fired because we couldn't win under the circumstances that were there at Cal. I am proud that I was able to identify those men.

I've had some other tremendous assistant coaches during the years that I worked. I worked with some great coaches. When Ralph Wilson (former owner of the Buffalo Bills) was interviewing me for the Bills job, I remember telling him, "Mr. Wilson, it isn't just a good coach you need." You need a good coaching staff. That's so important. There are times when the head coach doesn't know as much in certain areas of the game as some of his assistants. Yes, there were some coaches I hired that maybe were mistakes, but not many, very few. There were one or two over the years that I could look back on and say no, this guy wasn't really what I had in mind. For the most part, I was very fortunate to work with some of the greats.

I was fortunate enough to work for a man who wasn't just the best general manager in the National Football League; I think he was the best general manager ever. That was Bill Polian. Bill and I worked together. We may have had strong opinions, sometimes even disagreed, but never in mean terms. We selected only people of high character for our team and for our coaching staff. I didn't want to mix up high character with personalities. Some might be very extroverted. Some might be more self-contained. Look at the difference in personalities between Vince Lombardi and Tom Landry. Both were great coaches. Then there was Bill Cowher and Tony Dungy. Both guys experienced great success. I never felt I was being stabbed in the back, so to speak, by any of the coaches. I was blessed with a very loyal staff. Maybe there was one coach who I fired and I felt was detrimental to what we were trying to achieve, but that was all.

Transition to Being a NFL Assistant Coach

I coached at William and Mary for five very memorable years. The guys down there were some of the greatest overachievers you can imagine, fantastic students, and very dedicated. I still remain close to them, but the move to pros, it's different. I anticipated it would be different. You have to make adjustments. "If you don't change with the times, the times are going to change you." I heard George Allen once say that, and he was so right. It was a change, but it was something you anticipate and you have to learn to make that adjustment. I was fortunate to join a good coaching staff headed by Jerry Williams. One year later I was with George Allen out in LA. He offered me, back then, a massive raise of $1,500.

Los Angeles Rams

There were some great players on the Rams, like Deacon Jones and Merlin Olsen. Roman Gabriel was the quarterback. We had a very good season, but George Allen and the owner did not get along at all, so he was fired at the end of that first season. Our whole staff went with him to the Washington Redskins the next year. We had a couple of very good seasons. The second season we went to the Super Bowl and played the undefeated Dolphins. We came close, but not close enough and lost 14-7. It was a wonderful experience for me to work for George Allen and with the coaches on his staff, like Ted Marchibroda, Tom Catlin, Boyd Dowler, and LaVern Torgeson, and Mike McCormack. I could keep going.

Super Bowl VII

That year we blocked 11 kicks. I say that proudly because I was the special teams coach. Going into the fourth quarter with about five minutes to go, the Dolphins were beating us 14-0. They were trying a field goal. The kick was blocked. Garo picked it up and saw one of his teammates open in the end zone, but when he let the pass go, it semi-slipped out of his hands, and Mike Bass picked it up and went 75 yards for a touchdown. We were back in the game.
It was 14-7, but that's the way it ended.

CFL

When I was an assistant with the Washington Redskins, I was offered the head job with the Montréal Alouettes. Being a head football coach in the pros sounded very interesting to me. It wasn't an easy decision, but I decided to take the opportunity. I had seen other coaches come out of Canada after great success there and succeed in the NFL, like Bud Grant. That wasn't the reason I went. I went because it was an opportunity to be a head coach on the pro level.

Certainly it is different; the strategies are different. I was very careful at selecting my staff. I found men who had experience in the CFL. It was very important that I hired several of them. You study the game, but when it comes down to it the exact same things that win in the NFL win in Canada. If you run, throw, block, tackle, catch, and kick better than your opponent, you're going to win. Sure there are different rules, but the fundamentals of the game are very much the same.

J.I. Albrecht, the general manager, said when he interviewed me, "Marv when you come up here, you can use 12 men on offense." I said, "Wow that sounds great."

I walked into his office one day after our first game and said, "You didn't tell me the other team's good, too J.I."

Our owner was a man named Sam Berger, a wonderful, renowned gentlemen and a lawyer. He had been a general in the Canadian Army during World War II. He was just a wonderful man. He went out and paid the biggest contract ever for Johnny Rogers, a Heisman Trophy Winner, and brought him to Canada. Johnny was a fantastically, talented athlete, but he had a lot of personal problems that finally made us let him go after a couple of years. He has since resolved those problems. I understand he's back at the University of Nebraska as an advisor to the students there and is very well thought of there. So I'm so pleased to hear that the pendulum did swing back in the right direction for Johnny.

When I went to Canada, good things happened there. The five years I was there, we went to the Grey Cup Championship three times, and won it twice. My final year there, we had a 41-6 victory in front of the biggest crowd in the history of the CFL. At that time, we played in Montréal's Olympic Stadium. Things were going very well. I had three NFL teams approach me about being a head coach. One of them, I felt, was a team that was getting very old. They had been near the top for a while, but they looked they were about to descend. The Chiefs also approached me and even though they had experienced some tough times, I thought they had a chance to ascend and get better. There wasn't much doubt in my mind that I wanted to take a head job in the NFL if offered. It came and that's when I made that move.

Kansas City Chiefs
When I went to Kansas City, they had just completed two or three consecutive seasons of being 2-14. I knew it was going to be a little bit an uphill battle. The first year we improved. We doubled our wins; we won four games. We kept improving a little bit incrementally. We won four the next year and then I think six the next. The next year, seven, then nine. Then the strike year hit and things didn't go well for us. It was my demise. I got fired, but a couple of years later, Lamar Hunt, the

owner of the Chiefs who I have a great regard for told me, "Marv, I think we made a mistake in letting you go." I told that very same story to Mr. Wilson of the Buffalo Bills during my interview with him and was hired there.

After the 1982 season, I was let go. I did a lot of broadcasting and television work in '83. I was hired by the Chicago Blitz in the USFL in '84. It was great to come back to my hometown, but then the league went out of business after '84. I was back doing radio and TV in '85. In '86, I came back to Montréal as Director of Football Operations and halfway through the season, I got a call from Bill Polian and Ralph Wilson in Buffalo inviting me down and the rest is history.

Joe Delaney
Joe Delaney, a young lad from Northeast Louisiana, was our running back with the Chiefs. I think he was a second round draft choice of ours. He wasn't very big as running backs go. I think he only weighed about 180 pounds. That's comparable to about 190 or 195 today, but Joe was unbelievable. He was a tremendously talented player and a wonderful family guy. After his second year, he was at home with his family and some little children fell in a sinkhole or a pond. Joe couldn't swim, but tried to save them. He saved one, but Joe and the other young person didn't make it. What a tragedy.

Buffalo Weather
This may come as a surprise. The average temperature in Chicago during the winter is about a degree or two colder than Buffalo. However, the snowfall in Buffalo is three times the amount you get in Chicago. That's because they're on the east side of the lake. The weather pattern comes across the lake, picks up snow and dumps it all on the city.

Our fans reveled in it and late in the season, it was always a big help to us. We used to have a mantra, one I learned from my father, the old Marine: "When it's too tough for them, it's just right for us." That was the way we used to treat the weather.

Buffalo Bills Organization

Bill Polian once said, "It's amazing what you can accomplish if no one cares who gets the credit." This is one of the most team-oriented organizations you could ever imagine. Everybody was important. For example, during the four Super Bowl games we went to, Ralph Wilson took every single person in the organization from the ladies that cleaned up at night, the switchboard operator, the security personnel to those games. He flew them down, paid for their hotel, meals, tickets, and they were part of it. He wanted it known, Bill Polian wanted it known, I wanted it known, and all our players did that everybody in that organization was fine. That's what led to the resilience it took for our guys to keep coming back from the crushing disappointment of losing those games and still finding our way back after what proved to be the impossible dream.

Scott Norwood Missed Field Goal In Super Bowl

Forty-seven yards off of grass, fewer than 50% of those are made, but nevertheless it went wide by a foot or two. I feel so much for Scott Norwood, a quiet, unassuming young man, another high character guy, a good family guy. Our players and fans rallied around him when we flew back into Buffalo. We were taken downtown to Lafayette Square and we came out on the balcony of City Hall. There were 30,000 people below chanting Scott's name. He was moved to tears and said, "You're the reason we'll be back next year." He was right."

Team Playing in Four Straight Super Bowls

I have to admit it's quite an accomplishment. I think it's even harder, to go back to four in a row after you've lost the previous one because many people would say what's the use after the second time and give up and throw in the towel. I remember on a call-in show after our second Super Bowl loss, one of our fans called in and said, "Coach, please don't go back next year. I can't take it. I can't stand the agony. I can't go to work on the Monday after." I said, "Sir, I understand your anguish. I share it, but I'm glad you're not on my team."

Motivating Players

The answer to motivating players is simple. Select only intrinsically, motivated players. Select guys who are hungering for instruction, who want to get better. Select guys who, if you do say something that's meaningful, they respond to it. That was the way we selected them. I used to say to them, "Don't tell me you have the will to win. Do you have the will to prepare? If you lack the will to prepare, you don't have the will to win," and our guys had it. There was great internal leadership on that team. We had Jim Kelly, Darryl Talley, Kent Hull, Steve Tasker; I could go on and on. I always hesitate to name three or four or five guys because I think I'll leave out so many more who deserve to be acknowledged that way.

Origin of Buffalo Bills No Huddle Offense
During the 1989 playoffs we were playing the Cleveland Browns before they moved to Baltimore. Going into the fourth quarter, we were losing by 18 points. In those days, there was no two-point conversion, it was only a single point. Eighteen points down going into the fourth quarter, we were not going to piddle-paddle. We said let's go to our two-minute drill right now and we did and marched down the field, scoring a touchdown. Now we're down by 11. Somehow we got the ball back, marched down again and scored a touchdown with about three minutes to play. Now we're down by four. We stopped them, got the ball again with about a minute and a half to go. All of this occurred while in the two-minute drill. The whole fourth quarter was a two-minute drill, fast tempo, fast pace.

We marched down the field and got down deep in their territory. One of our great running backs who was a great receiver, Ronnie Harmon, looked down at his feet to keep them in bounds in the end zone and dropped what would have been the winning touchdown pass. We lost the game, but as we're walking off the field after the game, Ted Marchibroda, our offensive coordinator and a former fine quarterback and Tom Bresnahan, our offensive line coach said, "Marv, how about making that our offense next year?" I said, "How come you guys are thinking the same thing I am?" So that was our style of offense, the no huddle, go quick offense.

The whole idea was that the opponent would not have time to substitute players. They won't have time to signal their calls in and we would wear their players out. Those were the advantages. One of the things you have to be willing to do is to pare your playbook down to less than half of what it would normally be, so the players can master it and get it quickly. You have to simplify the offense. Also, you're off the field very quickly so our defensive coaches weren't in love with the two-minute drill. In almost every close game it was a 20 minute time of possession for us and 40 minute time of possession for the opponents.

If we had a good comfortable lead, we would come out of the quick pace, no huddle. Say we had a 17-point lead early in the fourth, we'd slow it down and run the clock and so on. We might have a greater time of possession in games where we won by a comfortable margin.

Buffalo Bills Players
What great players we had. That again was the work of Bill Polian, and our Director of Player Personnel, John Butler, who later became general manager when Bill moved on, and so many of our scouting staff. We had great personnel. We stuck with guys for a while and developed them. We had some low round draft choices, guys like Andre Reed a fourth rounder, who was so great. Steve Tasker, who was put on waivers by the then Houston Oilers, the greatest special-team player ever. We had guys like Jim Kelly, Thurman Thomas, Bruce Smith, linebackers like Cornelius Bennett, Shane Conlin and Darryl Talley. What a group of guys. I remember them so.

I used to kid them a little bit. I said, "You guys have character and I've got to tell you there are a bunch of characters on this team." Again, it's not just the coach. It's not just the players. It's the owner and everybody else. After the greatest comeback game in the history of the NFL when we defeated the Houston Oilers in the playoffs after being down 35-3 in the second half, in the locker room after the game when all of the celebrating finally calmed down, I said to our players. "Hey guys, I want you to know that I just coached the greatest comeback in the history of the NFL, and I want you to know that I couldn't have done it without you." We had some great players.

The Comeback Against the Houston Oilers In Playoffs
That was one of the most memorable, playoffs. We played the game without three of our star players. Jim Kelly was injured. Cornelius Bennett was out injured, who was our great linebacker who didn't get the credit I think he deserved even now. Thurman Thomas was out injured. Still we came back from that tremendous deficit. It was an unbelievable experience.

Frank Reich led the greatest comeback in collegiate football history, and he led the greatest one in pro football history. That's amazing. There's another high character, talented guy. I never had a problem with him and Jim. They were very close in fact.

Pro Football Hall of Fame Induction
First of all, you wonder, am I really here? I never dreamed that this would occur when I first started the game. I wasn't a Pro Football Hall of Fame playing talent, but when I started coaching, it never even occurred to me that someday I might be up there with guys like Vince Lombardi and so many other guys. I still think about it. My initial expectancies couldn't have been very high by anyone who was predicting. I looked out at the audience at some of the great ones that were out there, from Chuck Bednarik and so many more. I saw them out there and the looks on their faces. 'Wow am I here?' That's the feeling you have. The Pro Football Hall of Fame is a very uplifting place to be. It was magnificently run by the previous executive directors and now by the current one, Steve Perry. It's always just a delight to go back and share memories and maybe a few exaggerations too, with some of the guys there.

Job of a Coach
Getting a team to play as a team and not as individual talents is a huge part of the coach's job. It starts with the type of players he brings on board. We were so aware that weren't going to bring a guy on board who had an attitude problem, who had a history of drug abuse, who was a distraction, or who was selfish. Now don't mix that up with personality. We had some guys that were bubbling extroverts and some that were more laid back, but they team oriented. They showed up for practice every day and they didn't place blame on their teammates. We tried to make sure they walked off the field every single day a little bit better off from what they learned in practice. Those were the kind of guys we were after.

Players
Most of the players are a lot smarter than you might think to tell you the truth. I just tried to be myself. Everybody should coach within themselves. I didn't try to impress them by being too intellectual. Once in a while they'd laugh because they thought I used a word that maybe

was not en vogue or not used very often. That's why jokingly, at one of my induction speeches at the Hall of Fame where a lot of our players were, I used a big word and said, "Look it up Thurman." He was sitting in the audience because he used to once in a while raise his eyebrows if I said something that sounded a little bit high blown but I communicated in my field well.

Best Coach He Coached Against
Don Shula was the best, but there were so many others. I think we competed as an assistant against Vince Lombardi, against Tom Landry. I can go on and on. There were many good ones. Bill Parcells we competed against, Marty Schottenheimer. I can go through a litany of names. There are a lot of good ones. There are none of them I don't respect. There are none of them that I dislike.

Coaching Philosophy
I told our players, "You don't get paid for Sunday, that's fun. Getting ready for Sunday, that's the work."

Buffalo Bills Head Coach Marv Levy prior to Super Bowl XXVII, Sunday, Jan. 31, 1993. Photograph copyright Associated Press

Chapter 5

Y.A. Tittle

> College:
> Louisiana State
>
> Career History:
> Baltimore Colts (AAFC) (1948–1949)
> Baltimore Colts (1950)
> San Francisco 49ers (1951–1960)
> New York Giants (1961–1964)
>
> 1971 Inductee Pro Football Hall of Fame

College Choice
Marco, Texas is my hometown. It's about 20 miles from the Louisiana border. I got scholarships to the University of Texas and LSU. My brother had lived in New Orleans, Louisiana. That is why I went down there. It was a good decision, I think.

LSU
LSU had a good team. We went to the Cotton Bowl in 1946 and played against Arkansas. We beat Alabama and all the Southeastern Conference schools during the season. I enjoyed it a lot.

Cotton Bowl Against Arkansas
The score was nothing-nothing. It's not too big an honor to not even score a point and be most valuable player. We made 19 first downs and Arkansas made 2. We played on ice. We just played in tennis shoes because we could not stand up in cleats. We could not score. We would get down around the 25, 30 yard line and it was solid ice. Nobody could stand up. We could not get across the goal line. It was nothing-nothing.

On a day like that you have to learn how to palm the ball a little bit. I took thumbtacks and I filed them down really low. Then I put them on my right fingers and thumb tips. Then I wrapped tape around my fingers. It was illegal to do that but at least I could puncture the ball with the thumbtacks a little bit and get a little friction. It was against the rules but I got away with it. I put tape around all the fingers on my left hand so the referee would not be suspicious.

I will tell you a little secret. I used those thumb tacks to my advantage. Some of those big tackles would get me and twist my arm and pinch me and do everything else. I had my weapon too. I had those thumbtacks. I could put my hand up under their elbow and run my hand up and down. I scratched the heck out of them. They did not know that until the game was over and they thawed out. They were so cold they did not feel it. I should not tell you that. I got my revenge.

Baltimore Colts
I was drafted by Baltimore. I went to the All American Conference and I played under a legendary football person. Cecil Isbell was the coach. He was a passing type coach. He had been an All-American at Purdue, I think. He believed in the forward pass. He encouraged me to become a good player, and taught me some of the skills of the forward passing game.

Baltimore folded financially and collapsed. We were redrafted. The Baltimore players were put in the college draft. We were redrafted like college players. I was San Francisco's first draft choice. I went to California. I played here ten years and got married, raised a family, and went into business. I am still here and I like it.

Frankie Albert
For the first couple of years I played behind Frankie Albert. He was good for me because he gave me some of the skills of quarterbacking. He was a very confident person. I do not want to be critical of him, but he was not a great thrower. He was a run around quarterback. He had good knowledge of the game and good leadership qualities. I learned a lot from Frank. He was a good friend. He and Fran Tarkenton invented the bootleg.

Alley Oop Pass

That was not an invention, that was if you can't find anybody open just throw it up in the air and let RC Owens jump for it. That did not take very much skill.

R.C. was a basketball player in college. He could really jump, rebound, get the ball, and get up high in the air. I was trying to throw the ball away one day out of the end zone. I threw it too short. R.C. jumped up in front of about five people and pulled it down. I gave him credit for it. He said he could do it every time, so I started doing it. We could not think of anything to call it. If I got in a huddle I would say, "Okay R.C. Alley Oop." That was the name of the play, R.C. Alley Oop. That took a lot of skill. You could do it. I could do it. My wife could do it. Throw the ball high up in the air and let R.C. jump for it. Players from the opposing team would try to get under the ball to try to intercept the pass and they would end up bumping into each other. R.C., he would swoop in at the last second between them. He would come down with a big hyper finish from the air and he would gobble the ball up.

R.C. said he liked the ball to wobble a little bit so he could judge it better. He did not want a tight spiral. He wanted it to wobble. I did not want to throw a wobble because you are proud of your ability to throw the ball with a tight spiral, and things like that are pretty. He came down with about three or four Alley Oops. I learned how to throw a nice wobble.

Trade to New York Giants

I had to make a decision as to whether I was going to quit playing. I had already played a long time in football before I was traded. I was married and had a young family. My wife's mother said she would help out with my two young children at that time when I went back to New York for training camp,. That made it possible for me to play some more.

Million Dollar Backfield

My only problem with the million dollar backfield was keeping track of who carries the ball three times or four times. I would try to make it even so that nobody would get mad. I had Hugh McElhenny, Joe Perry, and John Henry Johnson. They were something else.

Joe Perry carried it most of the time. He had a lot of stamina. McElhenny was never in condition too much. He could not carry the ball like Joe Perry, or as many times as Joe Perry. It worked out fine. McElhenny was a runaround type of guy. He would run right in, change his mind, go back to the left, back to the right. He did not want to carry the ball 25 times a game like Joe did. He could not because he was too exhausted, I guess.

I was a little bit jealous of them. But listen, I was the quarterback and my job was to win the games. If we could win the game with me throwing two passes, that was fine. It did not make any difference to me. All I wanted to do was just win. With Joe Perry, Hugh McElhenny, and John Henry Johnson, boy I could not make too many mistakes. The short passes I would throw to McElhenny and swing passes to John Henry. I had an opportunity to throw short in games for a lot of yards.

Let's put it this way, I did not, at the time, appreciate Red Hickey. He was a tough guy. Later, I learned to appreciate what he gave. He was a good football coach. He had talent. He had good skills. He knew a lot about the game and he was a demanding type of person. He was not popular with some of the players at the time. We learned to appreciate his talent.

Going to New York was an opportunity for me. My wife wanted me to go there because she wanted to go to stage shows. That is one of the reasons she wanted me to go. She was the best thing that ever happened in my career. I got recognition in the New York papers, the largest press in the world, and also the entertainment industry. We had a good team back then. We won the Eastern Conference four or five times in a row. That was a great break for me.

John Brodie
I am not sure John Brodie would have beat me out with San Francisco. I am joking I am not trying to make a case about that.

John Brodie was a great quarterback. There was no question. He had a good arm and good knowledge of the game. He turned out to be a great pro.

He was a great golfer but there was a rivalry. When two quarterbacks are equal in talent, there are going to be rivalries. There is going to be choosing up sides by teammates with some teammates pulling for one guy and some pulling for the other guy. It did create a problem with the team. Some of them were Tittle fans and some of them were Brodie fans. It was not a healthy thing. It was okay, but not the way it should be.

New York Giants
I know I had great years in New York. I know that when I came back to San Francisco to play against the 49ers after two years of being traded to the Giants. Boy, I turned it on. I had my big day.

Giants quarterback Charlie Conerly did not welcome me with opens arms at first, but we later became good friends. His wife and my wife were very close friends. After Charlie's retirement we became good friends. I saw him. He lived in Mississippi. He did not hold any anger toward me to his credit.

Throwing Seven Touchdown Passes Against Redskins In 1962
I think my best game as a pro was against the Washington Redskins in 1962. I threw seven touchdown passes. I forget how many yards but I think it was probably the best day I had in pro football.

I did not have any secret. I just had some great receivers. I just kept throwing. I was not shooting for a record, in fact, I never even knew I had broken a record till after the game was over. They told me I had broken the record. We would score and they would score. Then we would score again and they would come back. We would get ahead but they would come back again. I had to keep throwing so I ended up breaking the record accidentally.

Giants Offense
I had Frank Gifford and Kyle Rote. Kyle was a great player. But it was not like the million dollar backfield. I do not think in the history of pro football that a team had three running backs of that caliber.

Scrimmage
We did not scrimmage that much. Once a season starts you do not knock down scrimmages too much. You do not want to get any ball players hurt. In training camp, we would scrimmage. We had all out game type scrimmages. We had Sam Huff and Andy Robustelli. They were all on that defense. All the stars were defensive players.

Reason For Losing Three NFL Championship Games In A Row
I do not know any reason. Except I do know this, the games that we played, the championship games, the field should not have been played on. There was ice and snow. Ice, ice, and more ice. From the quarterback standpoint, you could not hold on to the football. You could not throw the ball, you had to sort of sidearm it and sling it because the ball was frozen. I am not trying to make an excuse. I am very disappointed I did not have any championship winning games. At least I got there many times. That is more than some quarterbacks could say.

Uniform Number
I wore number 64 before they changed the rules for numbers. Quarterback numbers were in the '60's originally. Frankie Albert was number 63 originally and then he was 13 after the change. I was 64 and when they changed I became 14.

Picture Of Him Kneeling On Field & Bleeding
I do not remember what I was feeling then because I was out. I did not know where I was. I think the score was 0-0. I am not sure. No one can score on an ice and snowfield. I got knocked coo-coo. That is a famous picture. You do not see my winning touchdown passes you just see me sitting there like I am praying to the good Lord.

Favorite Receivers
In New York, I had Del Shofner and Frank Gifford to throw to. Frank Gifford was a running back and I threw a lot of passes to him when he would come out of the backfield. I mean running and catching the ball. Del Shofner was a flanker and very fast receiver. He was my number one target in New York at first. In San Francisco, I had a number of guys to throw to like Hugh McElhenny. I threw it at a lot to running backs out here because we had Joe Perry, John Henry Johnson, and Hugh McElhenny.

Allie Sherman

Allie Sherman was a very creative coach, sort of ahead of his time. He sometimes had problems getting along with some of the ballplayers. He was very good to me. I liked Allie and he was, I will not say ahead of his time, but he was very progressive in his thinking. He believed in throwing the ball and we did that. He created a lot of new ideas.

There was some, I will not say disappointment, but some resentment. Allie was a new coach with new ideas. A lot of the team were Tom Landry players. They idolized Tom Landry. They always compared Allie Sherman to Tom Landry. I did not play when Tom Landry was there.

Movie "Any Given Sunday"

Oliver Stone contacted me and wanted to know would I play a cameo role in the film. I did not say too much. I did not do too much acting. I did a lot of coaching in the movie. When they got down to the end, they cut my words out because they paid you residuals on how much speaking you did. I remember saying, Send in the kicking team. That is about all I did. I was a great actor. Clark Gable would have been jealous of me.

Decision to Retire

First of all, I played on so many good teams. So many teams that won. For some reason, the New York Giants management or Allie Sherman, I do not know whether it was Allie or not, but they traded lots of the players away. We went from the top to the bottom in a hurry. I was 30 some odd years old and it was not time for me to start all over again and recharge the batteries anymore. I played 17 years and that was longer than anybody had ever played. It was time to quit, I guess. I will tell you the truth, I really was not finished. I could still throw better than any of the other quarterbacks they had.

They had a lot of quarterbacks that came long after me. We played what you called an Exes Game, where the old timers came back and played against the new team. I came back as an ex, an old timer. I ripped them apart. A quarterback is not like a running back. I do not have to worry about my legs giving away on me. I did not have any knees that hurt. Nothing was wrong with my knees. Nothing was wrong with anything.

My arms were still as strong as ever. I could still throw a ball 80 yards in the air when I quit. I could have played longer but my wife did not want me to. She thought it was time for me to hang it up. Sherman had traded a lot of players away. They were not going to be the New York Giants of old, they were rebuilding.

I mean, I quit when I had a lot of good years left. I had some great years in New York, and then we had a bad year so I decided to hang it up mainly because of my pride. Then when I went to the 49ers training camp the next year I got to coach the 49ers backfield. I was coaching, but the coaches were throwing the ball especially when we were working on our defense. I would throw and I was just ripping the defense apart. I was the best quarterback on the field, and I wanted to come back because the coach of 49ers said, If we can get you released from New York, would you play for us? John Brodie was ruled ineligible for some kind of a gambling bet. The Giants gave me the okay to go ahead and play if I wanted to, but my wife said no. She said "You've had a great career and the 49ers are not going to be as good of a team as you used to play for. You're going to lose a lot of things you want to remember, and don't do it." Anyway, she was my quarterback so she commanded me not to.

Pro Football Hall of Fame Induction
That was one of the great honors of my lifetime. When you are selected as one of the great players like Knute Rockne, Don Hudson, and all the other great players that is a great honor. There are still not too many quarterbacks in the Hall of Fame. It was a great honor and still is a great honor.

Name
My dad was Yelberton Abraham too. He was called Abe Tittle. I can't imagine him giving me my name. Yelberton Abraham Tittle Jr.

Yelberton Abraham was not my fondest name. Nobody ever knew my name. In high school or college, I kept it a secret. I was always just YA.

1963 NFL Championship Game
Well you know, I'm not going to make excuses because the Chicago Bears had a great team. But we were really a high scoring team in the

league at that time. I felt we could win in Chicago. We had been playing on good fields and with weather that was presentable and we were going to Chicago to play in the championship game. Now we're playing in ice and snow and mud. We weren't quite as adjusted to that type of weather as the Bears were. They had a great team, don't get me wrong. We had Sam Huff, Frank Gifford, Andy Robustelli. We had some wonderful players.

When I walked out I said, I hope I never see Chicago ever again. I don't want to ever think about cold weather ever again and the Chicago Bears is a dirty word.

New York Giant Y.A. Tittle squats on the field after being hit during a game against the Pittsburgh Steelers on September 20, 1964. Photograph copyright Associated Press

Chapter 6

Gino Marchetti

> College:
> San Francisco
>
> Career History:
> Dallas Texans (1952)
> Baltimore Colts (1953-1966)
>
> 1972 Inductee Pro Football Hall of Fame

Decision To Play Football
My family came from Italy and lived in West Virginia, where they worked in the coal mines. Eventually they moved to California to work in the steel mills. That's how we got to California. I settled in a little town called Antioch, where the population was only about 3,500.

My mother and father being from Italy, they didn't know much about football. When I started to play I had to fight them all the way. They didn't want me to play. They were afraid I'd get injured. They weren't very happy with me but I held something over their head. I said, "If I don't play football, I'm just not going to school. When I'm 16, I'm out of there."

They signed me up and they let me go out for Antioch High School. An interesting thing about that is when I was going out for football there, they had 24 uniforms. I didn't make the team but I still wanted to play. A friend of mine was the equipment manager of the football team. He gave me a pair of pants, shoulder pads, and I practiced with the team for the whole year, not going to any games, not being able to play, but I just tagged along you might say. Then my second year, I played a little and then third year I started to improve. That's where it all really started.

Enlisting in the Army

One day I left Antioch High School to go home, picked up my girl, and out of the blue I said I'm joining the Army. At 17, I started the paperwork to join the Army. My mother and father didn't like that so I gave them that same spiel, if you don't let me join I'm not going to school. They let me join and I joined the Army in 1944. From there I went to Mississippi and then I joined the 69th Infantry Division in Europe. That's where we got into action. I know they always say that I was in the Battle Of The Bulge. I was in part of it but by the time I got there, the bulge had been stopped and we started moving forward. Going into the Army was good for me because it gave me discipline and really, really kept me in shape. I think for every kid today, if they spent a year when they got out of high school in the service it would be good for them. I was over there for two years. I had enjoyed that.

College Choice

When I got out of the Army, I went back to Antioch and I wanted to play some football. I never thought of playing professional football because I wasn't that big. I organized a semi pro team and that was tough because you had to go around to the grocery store, the liquor store, the bars, and collect money for the uniforms. We did that and we had a pretty good team. My brother, who was a better football player than I was, played on the team. One day, we were driving to the Bay Area to play a team in San Francisco. As we were leaving the town, I noticed a red Chevrolet by my mother's house, so we stopped to see who it was. Inside the house, was a line coach from Modesto Junior College and Johnson, the head coach of their football team. They talked to my brother. They really wanted my brother to go to that college, so he committed to Modesto Junior College.

As we said our goodbyes, I shook the line coach's hand and he made a joke. He said, "You look like you're big enough to play. Why don't you come up?" I said I would, and I went there. My brother made first team right away. It took me about three weeks, and then I was recruited by Joe Kuharich and Brad Lynn to go to the university and play football. Then I went up to the University of San Francisco and things worked out well there. Then I ended up being drafted by Baltimore.

The first guy I met and the guy that really trying to get me in The University of San Francisco was a guy by the name of Brad Lynn. I don't know what school he went to. I can remember the day I was working in the bar and I was tending bar and all of a sudden this guy comes in with a suit and a tie. I wondered what he wanted because in that little town, most were working guys, guys going to shifts and coming home. He introduced himself. I said, What are you doing here?" He says, "We'd like you to come up to USF and try to play football for the University of San Francisco. At that time I was smoking a cigarette. I'll never forget I put that cigarette out because I didn't want him to think I was smoking. I reported to the University of San Francisco on the following Monday and went in to meet Joe Kuharich. At that time I was riding motorcycles and me and my friend drove up to San Francisco and went in to see Joe and he wasn't very impressed with me I guess because motorcycles drivers or riders have a bad reputation. We didn't have a bad reputation but I had a leather jacket on which everybody had to have if you were riding a motorcycle. You bought a leather jacket and on a leather jacket, the more zippers you had the better it was. You felt really cool. I had 17 zippers, one zipper on top of the other. Anyway, the meeting between Joe and I didn't go very well because I wasn't the Notre Dame type I guess that he was used to when he played there and he also coached a little there. Brad Lynn talked him into it. Brad Lynn said, "You don't whether that kid can play football."

We went out and Joe Kuharich was practicing the USF team from about I think January to June. There were full-scale scrimmages on Saturdays. I happened to go on this one particular day. It was on a Saturday and he got me the equipment and I worked out with them. Then when we went to scrimmage. He put me into the scrimmage. I wasn't dumb. I knew that they were going to try to run me, run over me, run inside, outside, or just to see if I had any ability at all. After that practice, Joe Kuharich told Brad Lynn, "You bring him in." That was my lucky day.

University of San Francisco
Most of the schools we were playing, the bigger schools had players play only on offense or defense but little schools like the University of San Francisco, we played both ways. We played Stanford once and Cal but most of opponents were all little Catholic schools like St. Mary's, Santa Clara, and that type.

We had nine guys off that one team that went into the professional level and made NFL teams. Our backfield at that time was Ollie Matson who is in the Hall of Fame. Ed Brown was the quarterback. Scooter Scudero was the other halfback and then there was Bob St. Clair, Dick Stanfel and one of the best football players on that team, I've said this a trillion times, was Burl Toler. He was a black athlete and he was a damn good one. He was probably the best athlete of all of us. Burl was drafted when he was a junior. We had some pretty good studs I guess.

Some of those guys, like myself, and there were a couple other guys I can't think of who were from the service. That's where a lot of the leadership on the team came from because the guys in the service were a little older than everybody else and realized how lucky we were to get another chance to play. We kept working pretty hard.

Burl Toler
I definitely think he'd have been a hall of famer, no question about it. I'd never seen a big guy, particularly on offensive. He had great balance. He had legs about the size of birds. He wasn't built that strong but he was strong and he played offensive tackle and he played middle linebacker and did an excellent job. He was the only one of us that started the all-star game mainly because when you go to those all-star games, a lot of times they got Big Ten coaches, Pac Ten; they got all the big schools and here you are from USF. The coaches always took care of their guys. On the first or second play in the college all-star game, the Rams ran a sweep around his side and he took everything down, stopped the play but the problem is he didn't get up. He tore up his knee terrible. In the locker room after, I was standing there talking to Kuharich and Burl was coming out of the shower and I said, "How do you feel, Burl?" He said, "I don't know. I don't think I'm going to make it." He took a step and his knee just went. He fell completely down. He never did recover from that knee injury. They didn't have much experience in those days on torn ligaments and that type of thing. That's what he had. That ruined his professional career. He would've been in the tops. He was voted captain, one of the greatest individuals you'll ever meet.

Team Turning Down Chance To Play In Bowl Game
The thing that led up to it is our senior year, we were undefeated and we were coming up to the last big game on our schedule and that was

against the College of Pacific. They had Eddie LeBaron. He played four or five years as a pro. He was a quarterback and they were undefeated. We played them and we beat them 47 to 0 or something like that. We really gave them a whooping. Then the bowl representatives came down to the locker room after the game. I don't know whether they were looking at us, or College of Pacific because they were awfully good also. The way we manhandled College of Pacific that afternoon I guess they decided to take us. The only problem they had, they wanted us to go and leave Burl Toler and Ollie Matson our black players at home. When they asked me about it, I said "Hell no. They're a part of this team." I was the captain too. I said, "If they don't go, we don't go, I don't go. I don't care." The whole team took that approach that we would not go without the whole team. What was really great about it is that everybody stood together on it. You didn't hear one guy upset saying we should go, we'll never get another chance, or that type of stuff. Never heard it. When we said we weren't going, that was it. The subject was dropped, and we never regretted that decision. That's they way things go.

It was tough in those days for black athletes I guess. I never knew that because in California it was never really a problem. Professionally, it was tough on them because a lot of places where we went down south to play, the black athletes had to go into a different part of town to stay than where we were. We couldn't stay together. We didn't like that. I didn't like that but there was nothing we could do about it.

Draft
I never thought that I could ever make a professional team because of my size. I was tall, 6'5 or 6'6 but I only weighed 215 to 220. People think during the early years of professional football players weren't big. I'll tell you one thing, they were big. They drafted guys because of their size or whatever. They drafted me and I only weighed like I said, 220. When I reported to camp, I used to, when they had weigh-ins put a 10 pound weight in my jockstrap so I'd weigh 230-235. They'd look at me a little better I guess. Eventually I could throw away the weight. I made it and it wasn't a very good season. We were terrible but I got to play.

We moved to Baltimore and the fans were great to us. I think our team was great to the fans too because we used to out and sign autographs every night practically and do those types of things that other teams would never do.

Baltimore Colts Defense
We had a great defensive team I think mainly because we didn't blitz much. We could rush the passer and we could cover the run and screens and really, really play well. The defense had Art Donovan who of course is in the Hall of Fame. Then there was Big Daddy Lipscomb, who was 6'7 and about 300 pounds. We had a guy named Don Joyce, Ordell Braase who was an excellent defensive end, and me. We had a great middle linebacker in Bill Pellington. We got everything done that we wanted to do in a game just with those guys. We didn't have to blitz. Some players are lucky if they play with a team who blitz almost 40% of the time. That gives you a lot more chances to get sacks. We played a regular defense and we got a pass rush and everything else. Offensively, you couldn't find a better receiver than Raymond Berry, a better halfback than Lenny Moore, L.G. Dupre was there at fullback, and Johnny Unitas played quarterback. He was as good of a quarterback as ever played the game. Not only that but he was one of the nicest guys that we had on our team. I shouldn't say it like that because every guy on our club was really, really nice. There was no dissension. We all got along good and it was a lot of fun. I didn't make much money but it was a hell of a lot of fun playing in Baltimore.

Weeb Ewbank
When I reported to the Texans, they had a coach named Jimmy Phelan and I don't know if he ever knew what football was. We worked hard but never saw a film. Our meetings were short. It was just a poorly run organization. As a matter of fact, we only stayed in that town five games and they declared bankruptcy and we were a traveling team them. We lived in Hershey and stayed at the Hershey hotels and would go to work every day and then play all of our games.

Art Donovan's Diet
Art Donovan's diet was hamburgers, hotdogs, Jewish bologna or whatever they call it, spaghetti and pizza. That was his diet. I've never seen him eat a salad or vegetables. That was his dinner. Them days, what they did was weigh you in every week. They would weigh you in and give you a weight to be. We'd get a letter during the off-season

telling you report to camp ready to hit and do this and do that and by the way, we want you to report at 240. I had a weight of 240. I was 20 pounds under. That's why I went in with the weight in my pants. Arty, he weighed about 286 but during the weigh-in, he would starve himself until he reached a weight that they wanted him at 277. What was tough about that, they'd never tell you what day that they're going to weigh you on. So the guys that had a weight problem, hardly ate until they got weighed in. During the weigh in of course, Arty weighed in at 277 but by the time we got to the game on Sunday, he was probably 285. They pumped themselves up with food or liquids.

Colts Players Chicken Eating Contest
Art Donovan tells all these stories over and over and each time he tells a story, he gets one part from there, over here, one part from over there. He is always funny but he may tell the same story five different ways. Don Joyce was the champ of the eating contests, of eating period. We were talking and we just ate a lot of chicken. We weren't having any contest because I would never challenge him because I could never beat him.

1958 NFL Championship Game
You got to love that game because it made professional football. It made it because that was the only game in NFL history that ended up in a tie. The thing that was funny about that is when the game ended in a tie, we didn't know, the coaches didn't know, and I guess the ownership didn't know what are we going to do. You can't end a championship game in a tie. It has never been done. Then that's when the word came down because Commissioner Bert Bell was at the game and he said, "We'll play and the first score wins." That's what we did. As far as the greatest game ever played, I really didn't think it was. I think there were a lot of mistakes made. I think Frank Gifford fumbled two or three times. We fumbled twice. The ending was exciting.

They proved on the big screen that Frank Gifford was stopped short of a first down. Some scientist that had a way of measuring, taking measurements with a laser light went through the whole play, where Frank went down and where the yard line was before. He was nine inches short. Frank always tells me "You know Gino, I made that first down." I said, "Frank, who's got the ring? We got the ring." That shut him up a little bit.

The newspapers in New York were on strike. I'll tell you this, I think if that game was played in Baltimore, it would've been great for us but it would have never got the coverage that the New York press and radio and television gave it. That's what pushed it over the hill, man. After that, the next season, all the stadiums that were half full or three quarters full the previous season were all full. Tickets were starting to get hard to get. New York made it. The players gave me the game ball.

Bob St. Clair
Playing against him was a strange feeling. At USF we'd hit each other every day and then have a couple beers. We were pretty good friends and then professionally it was completely different. I wouldn't talk to him before a game. He wouldn't talk to me. It was just all business. It wasn't all laughing.

You go to some of these games now, they hate each other. We never did that. It was a serious, serious situation. I played a game without talking. If he held me I'd kick him or something. After the game, we'd see each other. If he had a couple hours to spare we would go and have a couple beers and talk a little bit about the game or whatever and then he'd go back to San Francisco and I'd go back to Baltimore. I would never pat him on the butt and tell him he did a good job.

Pete Rozelle At University of San Francisco
I'd say he was as good as our best player. He couldn't be more polite to us. If we wanted something, we'd ask him, he fought like hell to get it. He was just a hell of a nice guy.

The only thing, this is just kidding, the only thing I really didn't like about what he did; one day they called, Ed Brown, Ollie Matson, and me to Joe Kuharich office. Coach Kuharich wanted to see us.. He talked to us and said, "I just want you guys to know that we're going to play Florida this week and it's up in New York."

He said, "We've decided that we're going to push Ollie Matson for All-American." We went to New York. Ollie received the kickoff, and almost ran it all the way down for a touchdown. He had a super game. He really deserved everything that he got. The thing that Pete Roselle gave him was The Catholic All-American Plaque.

About four or five days later, Pete Roselle wants to see me so I go up and see him. He said, "Gino, here." He reaches in the drawer and gives me my plaque. I said, "Oh, thank you," and walked out. When he gave it to Ollie, man they must have had 15 guys from the press. I thought it was funny.

Pro Football Hall of Fame Induction
I felt great. Where I came from, the things that I had personally gone through, and not really planning on being inducted. Some guys say I'm going to do this, I'm going to do that, I'll be this. I never had any goals. It just seemed like where my right foot went, my left foot followed. I just never planned on going to USF, never though I'd play at a professional level, and never thought I'd be in the Hall of Fame. It's just been a great, great, great ride. What can you say? The people, the fans, the players I met really, really made it a good feeling.

Three Retirements From Football
The first time I came back I don't know mentally if I was ready to retire. I didn't report to camp because I was going to stay retired. I didn't stay retired because of one thing, Don Shula was named the coach. He wanted me to be a player coach so I said okay. I came back for that.

Then the second time I thought the team was ready maybe to go for another championship. I had retired and the guy that was supposed to take over my position was Don Thompson. They weren't happy with what he was doing so they called me back. I felt good that they wanted me but I really didn't want to come back because I didn't want to play the game. I didn't want to be, what's that quarterback from Green Bay that retired 30 times or whatever his name is. I didn't want to play that game. I didn't do it. Then after about three or four exhibition games, Thompson wasn't making them happy. They called me back. Shula had called me back and at that time I was still pretty much in shape. The Colts were so good to me. I couldn't say no, so I did it.

The last time I came back was in 1966, when Shula was going for the championship. Everybody was hurt so he asked me if I would come back. I was still in pretty good shape. I had been out of football for a year and a half. It was halfway through the season when he asked me to come back. So I went back and that was it. That time when I went home I said to Shula, "Don't call me anymore."

Don Shula
We knew that he was going to be a Hall of Fame coach. Everybody knew that because hell, when he got traded to Baltimore, he practically coached the defense. Charlie Winner, Coach Weeb Ewbank's son-in-law, was the defensive coordinator and didn't know a hell of a lot about the professional way of doing things. Shula used to teach him. We knew that Shula would become a very fine coach. As a player, he was not a great player but capable because he was so smart that he knew the patterns of the opposition we were playing and all that. He was a good player but he didn't have the speed like a lot of the guys had, but he did a damn good job and mostly because of his abilities to know the defenses.

Comparing Weeb Ewbank & Don Shula
When Weeb came in, he brought organization and Weeb was a very, very smart offensive planner, game planner, recruiter, drafter. He knew everything from A to Z about football, which made him successful. He had one major flaw and I told him this. I'm not saying anything behind his back. I told him that he was too nice.

He didn't like Alan Ameche. Nobody knew why he didn't like Alan. Alan knew he didn't like him. For some reason, he didn't like him. He would pick players that he didn't like and it would be obvious.

Eventually players on the team start to loosen up because they knew that, like me for instance, I could probably do what I wanted to do and Weeb wouldn't have said anything to me. If the third stringer made a mistake and John Unitas made that same mistake, he would chew the third string quarterback out but wouldn't say anything to John. That type of stuff just doesn't go. Eventually the football players will take advantage and they did after five or six years. He lost his job coaching with the Colts and if you look at his record when he went to the Jets, after five or six years he lost his job there because those guys did the same thing. They're making money and having a lot of fun. You just have to control them. He just didn't do that.

Don Shula, on the other hand, he would chew you out if you made a mistake. He didn't care who you were. He lasted longer as a head coach. The players might not have liked him. They would tell you this as I would tell you. I didn't like a lot of things he would do, but I had the respect for him. I didn't have quite the same respect for Weeb as a head coach as I did Shula. Shula was tough. The good thing about it, he always forgot. It's like the old saying, if you forgive, you got to forget it. You can't carry it around with you every day. You just got to let it go.

Baltimore Colt Gino Marchetti with Head Coach Don Shula. Photograph copyright Associated Press

Chapter 7

Jack Butler

> College:
> St. Bonaventure University
>
> Career History:
> Pittsburgh Steelers (1951–1959)
>
> 2012 Inductee Pro Football Hall of Fame

Pro Football Hall of Fame Induction
To be quite truthful with you, I never even thought about it. That was not one of my priorities. It's an honor and it's a privilege and all that, but I just look at it like I was fortunate enough that I had the talent to play the game and I enjoyed playing the game. I had a lot of fun and it was great. The rest of it was a bonus that's thrown in. I never thought about it and that's all there is to it.

St. Bonaventure
I love the city of Pittsburgh. I was born and raised here and went to St. Bonnies, which is only like a four-hour drive from Pittsburgh. I went there and had a great time. I moved back to the city and I plan on staying here the rest of my life.

I never played high school football. I wasn't that big. At that time, I was probably 5'10" or 5'11" and 160 pounds. Now I went to St. Bonnies, I was only 17, and got to be 6-foot and 200 pounds.

My father was friends with Mr. Art Rooney who owned the Pittsburgh Steelers Ball Club. I just finished high school. I was talking to Mr. Rooney and he said "I know some people down at Virginia Military Institute. That's a good school and you ought to go to VMI."

I went home and my father said, "Well, okay, yes, that's alright." I'm thinking, I don't want to go to a damn military school. I said, "I don't want to go to VMI. It's a military school and I don't want to be a soldier or anything."

I went back and saw old Mr. Rooney and told him I didn't want to go to VMI. He said, "My brother is up at St. Bonnie's, Fr. Silas Rooney, the athletic director at St. Bonnie's." He said, "That's a nice little school. You want to go to St. Bonnie's?" I said, "Yes, that'd be fine. Anything's better than VMI."

So I went to St. Bonnie's. I didn't know where it was. I didn't know anything about it. I went up there and that was all there was to it. It was a nice little school, nice campus and everything, and I thought it was great.

When I went there, I happened to be put in a room with two other guys and they were both scholarship football players. That's all they talked about. They talked me into going out for football. I went over with them. The equipment manager had a tablet with everybody's name on it. I'm behind these guys and we're training. He looks at the list, and said, "You're not on this list. Hit the road."

I left and I happened to bump into Fr. Silas Rooney, the Athletic Director. He told me to go back down the next day and I did. They gave me a uniform and that was the beginning of it all.

I had no position. I never played the game before. They put you in a big long line. The scholarship football players, they knew who they were. Then there were a lot of walk-ons and things, and I was like a walk-on, whatever you want to call it. We're just standing in a long row and he'd come along and ask you what you played. The guy next to me was an offensive lineman and he said, "I'm an offensive lineman." I'm next in line. He said, "What do you play?" I didn't play anything. I told him I was an offensive lineman. They looked at me and said, "You'll never make it." I was probably about 170 pounds or something.

I sat around for weeks and weeks then a guy got hurt and they called for a defensive back. Nobody went in. They called again and again. I finally walked over and the guy said, "I thought you were a lineman." I said, "No, I'm defensive back." He said, "Get in there." That was it.

You just learn. You watch other people. I remember when they passed out the uniforms, I didn't know you put the pads inside the pants and everything. I had to watch them and I did the same thing they did, and put the pads on. I didn't know what they were. It was a brand new experience, everything.

I just watched. Whatever they did, I did. When the guy wanted a defensive back and nobody went out, I went out. I just watched the guy on the other side. Where he'd lined up, I lined across from him. You chase a guy, cover a guy, I knew that much. You just learn by watching and trying to do it.

Draft
I was not drafted. We weren't a big school. I graduated and I went home. I was going to go back to school. I was in graduate school, my last semester, and I was going to go back and get a master's degree.

Then that summer, the general manager of the Pittsburgh Steelers, called me up and asked me to come downtown. I went and met him. He asked me if I wanted to try out for the team and I told him, "Yes, fine. I'll try out." I was in his office and he pulled out a contract. He said, "Sign it." I said, "Well, how much will I make if I make the team?" He told me, $4,000. I told him I'd like to make $5,000. He said, "Sign the contract." In other words, sign the contract or get the heck out. I signed the contract.

I made $4,000 as a 21-years-old. I thought I was making an awful lot of money. That was plenty of money then I guess, for a young guy who still lived at home and had no expenses. Wow. I was in good shape.

Pittsburgh Steelers
They were still playing the single-wing and I didn't even know what it was. I never saw it before in my life. I never even heard of it. When I went to training camp, they were lining up in an unbalanced line. I'm looking at it and I'm trying to figure what is this thing. I'm a receiver. I

thought I was a receiver anyway. I'm thinking, there's no way in the world I can make this team. I'm not that big.

I go to Coach John Michelosen who was the head coach at the time and I said, "I'm quitting. I don't understand it, this single-wing, the formation. I don't understand it. I don't know how to play it. I'm a wide receiver. I thought I was a receiver. I'm going to go to Detroit and I think I can make the team there because one of my coaches in college is now a coach with the Lions in Detroit."

This coach told me to come to Detroit and he thought I could make their ball club. I told Coach Michelosen, I'm going to quit. I'm going to go to Detroit. He said, "You can't do anything until I cut you. You're under contract. That's it. You can't do a thing until I let you go."

I said, "When will you let me go?" He said, "I don't know. Just go out and do the best you can. I don't know." I figured I'm not going to make it anyway so I figured the hell with it. I will go all out. I'm hitting anything that moves. I'm doing everything. I made the damn team. I never thought I would with the single-wing. Then he changed me over to a defensive back.

It was better than trying to be an end on a single-wing, on the short side. Those other guys were as big as the tackles. They were big people. Like I said, I'm probably 6-foot. I was probably at that time maybe 190 pounds.

It was the second game of the season and we were playing the 49ers at Forbes Field. I'm just sitting on the bench. I thought I'd never get in the game. A guy gets hurt so Coach Michelosen says, "Butler, you get in there." I go in and at that time, I was playing different positions. In fact, I was like the third defensive end. He had Bill McPeak, and I was like the third defensive end and I played a little bit of defensive back during practice and things. He says, "Get in there." I go in and there's Howard Hartley, a defensive back who is hurt. I come back out and I say, "Coach, Howard Hartley's hurt. He's a defensive back." He said, "I know who's hurt. You get in there. That's when I become a defensive back."

They had some receivers who could run like heck, too, but I knew one thing. Nobody got up behind me in that game. I played so deep, they couldn't get behind me. They caught a bunch in front of me, but they didn't get behind me. Of course, that was the first time I was playing defensive back. They weren't going to score a touchdown on me. Oh, well. Those were the good old days, I guess.

Intercepting Passes
I think it's all instinct. You know your game. I think that was probably one of my best assets. I thought I had pretty good instincts for the game. I believed I could always catch the ball.

When I was in school, I was a wide receiver at St. Bonnie's and I thought I should've been a wide receiver. I still think I should've been a wide receiver. I could catch the ball; everything turned out well though. Being a defensive back was altogether different.

Ted Marchibroda & Jim Finks
Ted Marchibroda and I went to school together at St. Bonnie's. I was a year or two ahead of him. When I came to Pittsburgh, he came the following year or something. They drafted him and he came down to St. Bonnie's and we were friends all through college and everything.

Jim Finks was a good quarterback. He was smart and so was Ted. I'm not saying he was smarter than Ted or anything, but Jim Finks was smart. He handled people. He had a great personality. He could get people to do things, but he didn't have a real rifle of an arm. His passes were more of a floater. He had good accuracy, but he didn't have a lot of fire on the ball. Ted Marchibroda didn't either. Some guys could really throw the ball in fact some threw too hard. Ted and Jim were good solid quarterbacks.

John Unitas
John Unitas, is from Pittsburgh also. He went to the University of Louisville. I remember driving back to camp with Johnny. The coach said we could bring our cars back because we were going to break camp. It was toward the end of training period and getting down to the final cuts. We're driving back and John says, "I think they're going to cut

me." I said, "No, I don't think so, John. They never gave you a look yet. They never put you in any games."
He could throw the hell out of the ball. He'd stay after practice and I used to stay out and run past the defender just for the heck of it.

We got back from Pittsburgh, where we had played a preseason game. We were going to break camp that following week. We get back, and as we were walking over, here comes the head coach, Walt Kiesling. He calls John over and cuts him right then and there. He could've done that in Pittsburgh. Now John had to take a bus all the way back to Pittsburgh. He went to Baltimore and turned out to be one of the great quarterbacks in the league.

He never had a shot. He never got in a pre-season game and he didn't even practice. He didn't do much. I used to stay after practice and just run past the defender even though I was a defensive back. He'd throw the ball. He'd stay out there for hours just to get some time in. They didn't do anything with him and then they finally just cut him. Baltimore picked him up and wow that was it.

BLETSO
I went to Buffalo in 1960, as a coach and was on crutches. I couldn't do the job and I go to the owner and tell him, "Hey, you're paying me. I can't do the job. I'm on crutches and the doctors say I'm going to be on these for a long time. How can I coach, you know what I mean? Being on the field. There's no way."

I went back to Pittsburgh and I got into personnel. Detroit, Pittsburgh and Philadelphia formed a group called LESTO and they broke the country into areas. Each team put in two guys. They broke the country into six areas, and you covered all the schools in the area and made reports. The reports went to all the teams. Then they made me in charge of it.
Then I got Miami, Chicago, Baltimore to join and we end up calling it BLETSO. Then we got the Vikings to join. We put a V behind BLETSO for the Vikings and called it BLETSO-V and that's how it all came about.

I never really found a player. I happened to be in charge of it. I would go out with a guy for maybe two or three days. I would visit each one of them in the Spring and in the Fall. I would see how they went out and how they met the coaches and handled themselves. I would get all the reports back and read all the reports. Then we computerized everything. I never really went out and scouted guys and wrote guys up.

NFL Combine
In fact, we started the NFL Combine. Each team was bringing players in to give them a physical. Pittsburgh would bring guys in from the West Coast, give them a physical, and they'd go home. Then maybe Detroit would bring them in for a physical. They were doing all that.

I'm thinking that's kind of stupid. Why don't we bring the players in one place and get all the teams to join it rather than the teams doing that stuff individually. We would have it at Indianapolis and use their dome out there and each team would come with their own doctors and examine everyone they want to examine and work them out. We did and everything went great. It had to be about 1963 or 1964 when we started it.

Wonderlic Tests
We gave them. I didn't like them personally. That doesn't mean a player can't play football. We had to do it, but I don't know about it.

Scouting
A lot of it's natural, instinct and things. You play the game and you have to like to play the game and want to play the game. Those intrinsic things are important. Some guys have a lot of talent and you look at them, you work them out, you bring them to Indianapolis, they're in their shorts and they're built great, and they could run like hell, they could do everything, but they can't play football very well. They look great and everything. They look good, but they're not football players though.

Some guy looks the opposite and you say, "Holy man, the guy's a good football player. He may have stumpy legs and he may be a little overweight, but you think, 'Well, man, he can't be …' Then you find out he's a better football player than those other guys."

Photograph copyright Associated Press

Chapter 8

Hugh McElhenny

> College:
> Washington
>
> Career History:
> San Francisco 49ers (1952-1960)
> Minnesota Vikings (1961-1962)
> New York Giants (1963)
> Detroit Lions (1964)
>
> 1970 Inductee Pro Football Hall of Fame

College Choice
I was at USC on an extension. I lasted two months. My job was to water the quad where the Trojan horse is along with some flowers. I had to water that three times a day. Well, I did that for two months, but I never got my $65 and that's when I quit and I went to Compton J.C.

Washington paid me the most money. I can't really remember how much. My wife would. We had just got married on March 19, 1949. Her father wouldn't okay the marriage because I didn't have a job. I had just got out of Compton Junior College after having an outstanding year. The University of Washington propositioned me to go up to school. They made it possible for me to provide for my wife and get a college education. So, I went to the University of Washington.

I don't know how I got the money, but I got a check that was never signed by the same person each month. When I turned 21, I worked at the racetrack as a ticket taker and then my last two summers, I worked for Rainier Brewery. I was a public relations goodwill person. My job was to entice grocery stores, bars and restaurants to use Rainier Beer.

One of the first assignments they gave me, was on 1st Avenue and Seattle; I guess a low-income type area. So I'd go into the bar and introduce myself and say can I buy you a beer. I would offer everybody a beer. They gave me $100 to buy the beers and to influence the people to buy Rainier Beer. I made ten stops along there. I never had a beer myself, but when I was through, I came back to the office and gave them $100 back since no one made me pay for them.

I ended up keeping the $100. After I gave it back to them, they gave the money back to me. It kind of went like that.

Washington
Well, they had a new coach, Howie Odell. It was just like going to any other school or any other football program. They treated me very well. The practices were very difficult. It seemed like our practices were always on muddy fields; very seldom on a dry field. But it's amazing. I don't remember really playing a rainy game in the three years I played at the University of Washington. The only rainy days I had on a football field were at the University of California and Southern California.

Don Heinrich
Don Heinrich was kind of a quiet type of guy, a very confident individual. He was, for a young age, very intelligent about the game of football. He knew how to handle it. He had separated his shoulder my senior year. So he didn't play. He was an All American 1950 and '52. He had a separated shoulder in '51. He was just a natural. He was a good thinker, never got frazzled. He was just a solid quarterback. He ended up coaching in the pro ranks for some 20, 22, 25 years.

Draft
I could have gone into pro football back in 1949 after I finished one year at Compton J.C. The Los Angeles Rams, Hampton Pool didn't talk to me. He called my dad and wanted to meet my father. So Hampton came to the house and I was there. He offered me a contract at that time. I was still a minor so that's why he was talking to my father. He offered me, at that time, $10,000 to play for the Rams.

Of course my dad was very flattered and all that, but he turned Hampton Poole down. He said I was too young and would go to school. He wouldn't let me play.

The Rams were the team I always wanted to play for. In high school I was a ticket taker at the Los Angeles Coliseum for the Rams, UCLA, USC games, so I was really attached to the Rams. I was disappointed.

I was the eighth or ninth pick in the first round by the 49ers. I was hoping the Rams would choose me as their first choice, but they ended up getting the bonus choice and they took Bill Wade, a quarterback out of Vanderbilt.

It's hard to remember how it all came down. I played in the Hula Bowl. That's when they picked 15 outstanding college players in the United States and played against a few of the pros. I had an outstanding game and Frankie Albert was the quarterback for the Hawaiian team.

I guess Frankie had influence. He talked the 49ers into drafting me and that's how I got drafted by the 49ers, the influence that Frankie Albert had.

Rookie Year
I just came back from the College All Star Game in Chicago. Myself and Bob Toneff who was the 49ers second draft choice came back. We played the game on Friday night. Saturday we came back to San Francisco. The 49ers were playing the Cardinals at Candlestick Park. They gave us a uniform, suited us up, and we just kind of watched the game. It was sometime during the 4th quarter and Frankie Albert called a timeout. He came over to Buck Shaw and said put me in. I remember standing there and Buck says, he doesn't know the plays. He said, "That's okay, I have a play for him."
So I go into the game and just like old sandlot football, Frankie got down on his knees in the huddle and he drew what every player should do. It happened to be a 49 pitch and I went 38 or 40 yards for a touchdown.

The Chicago Bears game my rookie year I scored five touchdowns and two or three were called back. I broke the cardinal rule, you don't handle a punt within your own 10-yard line. You take the chances of it going in the end zone for a touchdown. I just caught it and it happened to work out and I went the distance for six points.

Nickname "The King"
Back in Chicago, after the game, everybody huddles around and the coach has a few words to say and so forth. Frankie Albert has the game ball and he says, "Hugh, we chose you as player of the game. Joe Perry you're still The Jet; Hugh, you're now The King, King Of the Halfbacks." And that's how he nicknamed me.

My Speed
In high school I held a world's record, 14 seconds flat in the high hurdles. I think I had the world's record in low hurdles; 220-yard lows at 21.6. I never ran the 100. I anchored a relay, high hurdles, low hurdles and the broad jump.

The University of Washington thought that I would participate in track, but I was never a really smart guy. I had all I could handle getting through school and playing football. If I ran track and football, I probably wouldn't have lasted three years at the University of Washington.

Pay In College
The three years I was in school, with my wife and I working we made more than $7,000 a year. It was great. The conference was checking on me every year. One time the conference came and asked where I got my car.

At Los Angeles Coliseum Relays in high school during my senior year I won the high hurdles, low hurdles, broad jump and our team took 4th in the relay. It was the last meet of the year and my mom and dad were waiting for me to come out of the coliseum. My mom, of course, gives me a big hug and a kiss and my dad, he just looks at me and smiled. He went to shake my hand and in his hand were the keys to my mom's car. It was a 1948 Dodge.

Supposedly he gave me the Dodge, but the thing is, they never took it out of my mother's name and when I drove up to Seattle to enter school,

I was getting parking tickets and I never thought much about them. Anyway, I never paid for a parking ticket. My mom was getting the bill. They paid my parking tickets for two years.

Million Dollar Backfield

I certainly was just a player. John Henry Johnson, he was up in Canada. He was playing somewhere up in Canada in 1952. They brought him down in 1953. It was Y. A. Tittle, Joe Perry, John Henry Johnson and myself. John Henry only played with us for two years before they traded him away. So the Million Dollar Backfield was 1953 to 1954.

Of course over the years, we all became Hall of Famers. But the story was, as I understand it, the Million Dollar Backfield was named because the 49ers were for sale in 1952. With Y.A., Joe, John Henry and myself, we started filling the stands. So therefore, Tony Morabito decided not to sell and he kept the club. The Million Dollar Backfield meant us selling tickets and so forth. That's kind of how it came about.

Reason For Not Winning A Championship

I hate to say it because there aren't many of them alive anymore, but we just never had a good defense. We could score on everybody, but we had trouble keeping people from scoring on us. Offensively, Jesus, for 12 games, I never carried the ball more than 15 times in a ball game as a 49ner.

Today, all these records that are being broke, geez, they're carrying the ball 20, 25 times a game. The percentages are the more you carry the ball the more opportunity you're going to have to make yards. The biggest problem, I think, was Y.A. Tittle. How does he share it? How does he share Joe Perry carrying the ball, me carrying the ball, and John Henry Johnson carrying the ball? That must have been a tough job for Y.A. I don't remember us ever talking about it, but if I was a quarterback, I would be thinking that. Who's productive today? It's tough for a quarterback to make decisions with three guys like us in the backfield.

Alley Oop Pass

That was an accident. Y.A. will tell you this too. The first Alley Oop was only maybe good for 20 yards for a touchdown. The ball slipped out of Y.A.'s hand and went high in the air and oop, R.C. Owens out jumped Jack Christiansen and Yale Lary, and caught the ball. That's how it came about. It was a fluke ball that went up in the air and R.C. Owens out jumped the other two players. So they went and then started practicing that during the week, because R.C. Owens could jump high and had good hands.

Frank Gifford
Frank Gifford and I became very, very, very good friends. Frank and Maxine were married. Peggy and I rented an apartment in the same complex. Peggy and I just had a baby, named Karen and two weeks later, Maxine had Jeff. We were in the same complex and so we became very close. We'd get together for lunch and dinner and potluck and that sort of thing for three or four months.

I was coming to play in the College All Star Game and Frank and I roomed together. Then we played in the East-West Shrine Game, we roomed together there. Then when I went back to New York to play for the Giants, he took me in. I roomed with him during training camp with the Giants. We were friends, he'd come to our house for dinner; we'd go to his house for dinner.

Then, of course, when I left New York, we all went different ways and we more or less lost contact. The only time we'd really seen each other was going back for the Enshrinement at the Hall of Fame. He doesn't make it every year and I certainly don't either. But I consider him a great friend and he's always been very kind to me. He always spoke very well on my behalf. He's just a great guy.

I knew when I was rooming with him with the Giants, he would be practicing and doing things for his radio show. He had a talk radio show at that time. Let's see, that's back in 1963. I consider him a great friend.

1963 NFL Championship Game
That was really disappointing. I can't remember too much. I took the second half kickoff and got to midfield and I made a move and I slipped on the ice. The defensive back was Roosevelt Taylor and he nailed me. But he was the last guy and if I would have gotten by him, it would have

been six points. That probably would have been the difference in the game. We lost 14 to 10 or something like that.

1961 Trade to Vikings
As a matter of fact, I was very unhappy. I can't really say what I think of Red Hickey. He was the worst coach I was ever around. Today, they could sue him for harassment. The way he treated some players, it was just terrible. The way he talked to them and so forth. I was supposedly considered one of his favorites, but we didn't get along. So I was very happy to be traded. I thought maybe I still had a couple good years in me, if I didn't get hurt. But to sell me for $15,000 that was a real insult to me. Red Hickey did that.

Norm Van Brocklin
He was a tough coach; I liked Dutch. He was tough on everybody, but he was really fair. If he didn't like something you did, like forgot your helmet, he'd come by and flick you in the head with his fingers. I really learned from Dutch in our meetings, like scouting for how we were going to play the team coming up, and so forth. I learned a heck of a lot from him and I understood more. I think for the first time I really understood what my position was supposed to be on a football field.

It seemed like before it was memorize the number, go to the direction and let your instincts take you wherever you want to go. I learned from Dutch that there were more things I could do to better myself and help the team.

Howard Cosell
I'm not saying this to offend anybody, but when I went into the Pro Football Hall of Fame, Howard Cosell came up and shook my hand. He was at Compton J.C. a couple years before I was, as a Public Information Director. He put his arm around me and whispered in my ear, "You are now the last of the Great White Hope." What does that tell you?

He was terrific. I think he had a lot of respect for me. That's the way I felt, the way he treated me, the way he talked to me, and the way I'd be invited to things. He chose me to toss the coin at Super Bowl XIX in San

Francisco. Of course, I didn't get to toss the coin. I had to tell President Reagan to please toss the coin.

We didn't talk much about anything when I went to Seattle. It was hard to try to bring pro football to the city of Seattle. Then he couldn't be close to me. We'd go to various meetings and he'd look at me, but he wouldn't wave or say anything. He couldn't have any direct contact with me.

Fran Tarkenton
It was obvious he was a scrambler. He was quick on his feet. He wasn't great with straight-ahead speed, but he was a good scrambler. Dutchman would have him work out with weights and throwing, developing his arm so he could throw the deep ball. He was accurate with the short ball, but you have to throw the ball further than 30 yards. I remember that. Certainly Fran went on and learned how to throw a ball more than 30 yards. He was great.

Pro Football Hall of Fame Induction
When I look back at my induction, and now we're celebrating the 50th anniversary of the Pro Football Hall of Fame, I can't believe it. Forty-three years ago when I went into the Hall, there were about 50 or 60 Hall of Famers at that time. God, we stayed in a motel. My mom and dad were there, my wife and my daughters. It seemed like we were scattered all over the place.

I remember it being fun because you had time to greet and see the other players that were in the Hall of Fame and that were going into the Hall of Fame. The day I went back for my 40th anniversary, I hardly knew anybody. They've all mostly passed away. There were maybe four or five that I would see that I remembered and played against, but when I went in the Hall of Fame, it was very simple. It was very close and very caring.

Today, it's a big show. It's a big deal in Canton and I'll tell you, the City of Canton, they do a fabulous job of handling all of us celebrities. I wish I could go back there and experience the first year I went in.

Secondly, one thing I disapprove of today is, all these speeches. Everybody thanks their brother's cousins, Uncle Jack and Bill and Bob, and they go on and on and on. It's obvious that anybody who goes into the Hall of Fame cannot properly recognize all the people that contributed to their success. I get blown away when all these guys get up there and spend a half hour talking about, a bunch of B.S. That's the only thing that frustrates me now. When we went in, we thanked our parents.

Photograph copyright Associated Press

Chapter 9

Don Shula

> College:
> John Carroll
>
> Career History:
> As Player:
> Cleveland Browns (1951–1952)
> Baltimore Colts (1953–1956)
> Washington Redskins (1957)
> As Coach:
> Detroit Lions (1960–1962)
> (Defensive Coordinator)
> Baltimore Colts (1963–1969)
> (Head Coach)
> Miami Dolphins (1970–1995)
> (Head Coach)
>
> 1997 Inductee Pro Football Hall of Fame

<u>College Choice</u>
When I got out of high school, all of the veterans were getting back from the service. They were getting all of the scholarships and I couldn't afford to go. I decided to stay out and work a year then go to college. I bumped into my old high school coach and he said, "Don't do that. You might not ever go." He said, "I know this coach at John Carroll who is looking for talent. I'll recommend you." He did and that's how I got to John Carroll.

I knew that Carl Taseff went to Cleveland East High School. When we were freshmen together at John Carroll, we got to be roommates and then became friends, lifetime friends. Carl was a great guy, a great football player.

NFL Draft
Actually, playing at John Carroll was right in the shadow of the Cleveland Browns. My senior year, we played Syracuse University in Cleveland Stadium. Paul Brown and his whole staff were there scouting Syracuse. We ended up winning the game. After that, Carl Taseff and I were drafted by the Browns.

Being selected was the furthest thing from our minds. As it turned out, I'm in this game when we beat Syracuse and we both had big days. That's the game that impressed Paul Brown and his coaching staff.

Paul Brown
Paul Brown was just a great coach, a great teacher. He just covered every possibility. There wasn't anything that he didn't prepare you for.

15 Player Trade
I was going to grad school in the off-season. I had some time between classes. I picked up the newspaper, opened the sports page, and my picture was on it. What's my picture doing in the paper? I looked and it said a trade, 10 for five, with the Colts. That's how I found out about it.

Weeb Ewbank
Weeb Ewbank was like a Paul Brown disciple. He used pretty much the same playbook and covered all the details. He was a great football coach.

Decision to Start Coaching
I played for seven years. When it became apparent that I was coming to the end of my career, I started to look at the possibility of getting into coaching. I was recommended to the new head coach at the University of Virginia, Dick Voris. He hired me over the phone.

Blanton Collier

Blanton Collier was just a genius of a football coach. I doubt if he ever played the game. He just was the guy that studied the game and was a great teacher, a lot like Paul Brown.

Becoming Colts Head Coach

Gino Marchetti was their captain and a great football player, a Hall of Famer. Carroll Rosenbloom loved him. Rosenbloom said to Marchetti that he was going to make a coaching change and asked, "Who should I hire?" Marchetti said, "Why don't you look into this young guy, Don Shula?" Rosenbloom said, "You mean the guy who played here who wasn't very good? Then he said, "Yeah, but he's a good coach."

I was in Detroit with the Lions at that time. Rosenbloom called and said, "You've been recommended. I think you're ready for the job." I said, "The only way that you'll find out is if you hire me." He liked that answer and hired me.

The toughest thing was coaching guys who I played with and the guys I played against. Now, all of a sudden, I'm up there and I'm their head coach. A lot of them were much better players than I ever was when I was a player. I had to convince them every meeting, every practice that this was the right thing to do and I knew what I was doing. Eventually, they bought into it.

Johnny Unitas

Johnny Unitas was unbelievable. The guy was tough mentally and tough physically. He could make the big plays in the big games. The guys were proven players. They were guys that were winners. You put them out there and they know how to win.

Leaving the Baltimore Colts for the Miami Dolphins

It was tough to do it. I love Baltimore. I love the fans and a lot of the things that were connected to Baltimore and the Colts. Miami was a great opportunity, a relatively new franchise with some very good players.

Achievements
I know the perfect season when we won all the games, 17 of them. It was a year to remember. I had a lot of great games to remember, but nobody had ever won 17 before.

There are a lot of things that I'm very proud of. I'm proud of the games I won as a coach, the perfect season, and back-to-back Super Bowls.

1985 Game vs. Bears vs. Dolphins
That's the best half of football I've ever been associated with. We had 33 points at halftime against a great Bear defense. It ended up we won the game handily. That ended up being the only game that the Bears lost that year. They ended up winning the Super Bowl.

Dan Marino had a great quick release and he did what he wanted to do with the ball. He had great decision making skills. We put him in situations where their safeties had to cover the slot receiver who at the time was a great slot receiver.

Johnny Unitas, Earl Morrall, Bob Griese, & Dan Marino
They had great talent. They were hard workers, had knowledge of the game, and were great competitors. You have to have all those things going for you when you accomplish everything that they did.

Earl Morrall
You never expect somebody to step in and do what Earl Morrall did. After Bob Griese went down, he led us to the championship game. Then, Griese was healthy again. I had to make a tough decision as to when I could put Griese back in, because Earl had been playing so well. Earl was a temporary quarterback and Griese was a quarterback here and now, and also in the future.

Coaching Key
When you have an arm like Marino, you want to put him in a position where he can use his great ability. Every defensive coach in the league would have congratulated me if I had Marino hand the ball off and not use his great arm. Coaching is all about analyzing your talent and putting them in a position where they can best use their talent.

David Woodley
We're in the Super Bowl with David Woodley. He was an athlete playing quarterback and Dan Marino was a quarterback playing quarterback. We got the most out of Woodley. Thinking back, he was a great competitor and that helped us win a lot of games.

Preparation For The Super Bowl
You use all of your experience and you try to use that and understand the pressures, the importance of the game, and how hard you worked to get there. You want to make sure that, when you get there, that you are ready to play the best game of your season.

Pro Football Hall of Fame Induction
That's just a great, great feeling to be recognized for your career and to go in there with so many people that have meant so much for the game, the hall of famers, and the people that were going in with me in that class. It's just a very, very special time in my life.

Greatest Player
You'd have to, I guess, have Jim Brown up there as one of the greatest players, if not the greatest player, then Otto Graham. I have so much respect for Otto. When he was a quarterback for the Browns, all he ever did was win championships. I've been around a lot of great players. My players here in Miami, like Dan Marino and the way that he threw the football, and all the excitement he brought to the game.

Baltimore Colts Head Coach Don Shula with Johnny Unitas. Photograph copyright Associated Press

Chapter 10

Doug Atkins

> College:
> Tennessee
>
> Career History:
> Cleveland Browns (1953-1954)
> Chicago Bears (1955-1966)
> New Orleans Saints (1967-1969)
>
> 1982 Inductee Pro Football Hall of Fame

<u>Mike Ditka & The 1963 Season</u>
It was in 1963 when he ran for that touchdown. If he hadn't scored that touchdown, we wouldn't have been in the championship. During the 1963 season, we had the last game, and we were tied with Detroit. He caught a touchdown. We kicked the field goal. We won. That put us in the playoffs.

<u>Tennessee</u>
I gave up basketball my sophomore year at Tennessee when I couldn't play both basketball and football. It was all football after that. It was my choice too.

Football was easier to play than basketball. In basketball you're traveling all over the place. Football is not quite as long and you're not on the field as long. You don't play as many games. You can just play those and get them out of the way.

Robert Neyland
Robert Neyland was one fine coach. He was a service man but he was a good football coach. That's why you can win with good people. That was a long time ago, back in the '50s.

Paul Brown
Paul Brown didn't like me. He sent me to Chicago. That was fine with me. I had some problem and I was out for a while. He just replaced me with some other guy. First of all, I had some kind of reaction. I had a sore throat and they give me something I had a reaction to. I lost about 20 pounds real quick there and I had a bad knee anyway for a little bit. When I lost all that weight during my second year, I finally played a game and I got benched. He put a guy named Massey in there, Carlton Massey. The second year, I don't know how many games I played before I got benched. I went down to probably about 230 pounds or something. It was my stomach or something. It was probably the best thing. The first year I couldn't do anything wrong and the second I couldn't do anything right.

Trade to Bears
I knew it was coming that year before it happened. He put somebody in there and took my place. It didn't make any difference. You got to go where you got to go.

Difference Between Paul Brown & George Halas
It was a little different. I was with Paul Brown with the Cleveland Browns first and he was just a completely different coach than George Halas. George Halas had been around so long. He started out in the old days. I got there and things were a lot different. Our drills in Cleveland were quick and to the point. We got Mondays and Tuesdays off which I liked with the Cleveland Browns. Unless you had an injury, then you had to show up. Our practices were not over an hour and 45 minutes on Wednesday and then they'd taper it down. We did things fast and quick and when the time was up, we'd be off the field.

With George Halas it'd be one more play, one more play. We'd probably be out there three hours by the time we got done because he didn't have anywhere else to go except the office. It was enjoyable for him to be out there. They had a bunch of old coaches. We never picked up any new coaches, any new blood until we got George Allen. It was the same old people.

We had weigh-ins. That was probably the toughest part of the practice. He set your weight, what he thought you were supposed to be. We'd line up like cattle and he'd put us on the big scale and weigh us every day instead of one day a week. We'd go to the heat baths and the whirlpools and everything and sweat it off. Then right after he'd weigh us, we'd make our weight and then we'd put the weight back on. We had a small dressing area downstairs. Then you went upstairs to get taped and everything was in a little room up there.

Coke At Halftime
During halftime of the games, we would always get a Coke. Dave Whitsell was sitting on a corner and someone came by with a Coke in his hand. Whitsell grabbed that Coke. He wouldn't turn it loose. They were fighting over that Coke, and finally Whitsell jerked it out of his hand and took a big chug of it and he spit it out. Guess what the problem was? That Coke had bourbon in it. He was carrying it to George Halas. That was his drink during halftime. That was the best interception he ever made.

George Allen
When we got George Allen, it helped us a lot. He did things a little different. He put us in different positions and it changed a whole lot of things. We got to change at times but you just can't do things one way one week, and do something different the next week. We got in this basic defense and things we could do off of that. When we had the other coach there, he had all this stuff. It would take all day to write it down. He had you going four places in one play. It's hard to do. George Allen was a fine coach.

Detective Agency
George Halas had the Burns Detective Agency following us. They would follow us after we left practice. They followed us as we went home. If Halas thought we were going somewhere else, he'd have us follow there. We found out later on that we were being followed. He had a lot of tricks I'll tell you. George Halas had to know what everybody thought about the team. The detectives would follow us to a

beer joint or most of the time we went to a bar at a hotel. They'd have that detective come in and ask us questions. This went on for a while and we finally found out.

One time I thought I was talking to the insurance man. He asked what do you think about Halas and I told him some things that weren't too nice. I answered all of his questions. Halas called me and told me what I said. He said "I want you to drive to my office after practice." He knew I wouldn't go downtown to his office. I said "I'm not about to drive downtown after practice and talk to you."

I said "You live at the Edgewater Beach Hotel right up from me how about just stopping by and seeing me?" He did. He stopped by, came in the door, and took his hat off. I was sitting there in a t-shirt. He looked at me and he said, "That's not your body. God gave that to you." I said, "Yeah it's a businessman like you to use, abuse, and trade, and do anything you want." He said "If you don't get out and drink anymore, I'll give you until the end of the season."

Jim Parker
Jim Parker from Baltimore was a real tough player. We had a pretty good time out there together. The first year I beat him pretty bad, and then he got a little smarter. He weighed about 290. He had a good team with him in Baltimore with Johnny Unitas, and a good blocking line. You had to go through him. There wasn't anywhere else to go. The other linemen were doing their job too. We had tough times with him.

Trade to New Orleans
It got a little tiresome in Chicago. I had three good years in New Orleans. I was hurt the second year. I got a little injured, but I enjoyed playing there. I had a good coach and it was different. We had a pretty good team. We played pretty good, but we didn't have enough players to do that good in New Orleans. We had some pretty good players, but we just weren't quite good enough.

Mike Ditka's Fight in Practice
The regular defense was on the sidelines. Our substitutes were in there working against the offense. The defense had a guy named Moon Mullen. He was a little defensive halfback. We noticed that there was a

little scuffle between Moon and Ditka and we were cheering for Moon Mullen to get him "Get him Moon!"

They had a little encounter there and I think Moon just swung at him or hit at him or something, and then Mike Ditka swung at Moon. Moon dodged it and Ditka fell down, and it looked like Moon punched him. His hands were going when he swung. The team gave it to Ditka. Ditka jumped up and said a little off colored word and walked off. Moon Mullen weighed 180 pounds and big old Ditka weighed about 220. That was something.

Pro Football Hall of Fame Induction
It was nice. I had to wait a long time but it didn't make any difference. I don't know why it took so long. People got different ideas. Sometimes they like some people better than others. I don't know. Like, why did Ditka have to wait so long for anything? He should've got in right away. He was a good football coach too. We needed him when Halas was there with his group.

George Halas & Finances
Back in those days when George Halas started, I didn't realize how tough he had it until I started reading a few books. When I read what they had to do back in the old days it was rough. He almost lost the club a few times. Halas and his whole family had to work. It was really a tough thing to do. He had about three brothers, and they all lived in the same place. He worked all the time and borrowed money.

One of the stories I read, was how one day Halas was working and after work he was going to play a baseball game somewhere in Chicago. Where he had to go, he had to take a boat with his team. That day he wasn't on time for the boat. The boat took off without him and it sank. Everyone on the boat died. His life was saved. They were a working group of people. I understood him after I read some of the books.

Retired Number
In New Orleans, they retired my number. But, when they sold the team, the new owner gave my retired number to one of his players. That's the way that some men do business. They're tricky.

Chicago Bear Doug Atkins tries to recover a fumble by Green Bay Packer Jim Taylor. Photograph copyright Associated Press

Chapter 11

Mike McCormack

College:
Kansas

Career History:
New York Yanks (1951)
Dallas Texans (1952)
Cleveland Browns (1954-1962)

As Coach:
Washington Redskins (1965-1972)
(Assistant coach)
Philadelphia Eagles (1973-1975)
(Head coach)
Cincinnati Bengals (1976-1979)
(Assistant coach)
Baltimore Colts (1980-1981)
(Head coach)
Seattle Seahawks (1982)
(Head coach)
Carolina Panthers (1993-1997)
(President and GM)

1984 Inductee Pro Football Hall of Fame

College Choice
Don Faurat came down and offered me a scholarship to Missouri, but so did George Sauer from Kansas. The proximity of Lawrence to Kansas City is about forty miles, and it's about 150 to Missouri.

Oklahoma did not come after me, to tell you the truth. I had several offers, but none from Missouri or Kansas, until it was in the paper that Bear Bryant invited me down to Kentucky and was going to offer me a scholarship. Then all of a sudden Missouri and Kansas got interested. I went to a Christian Brothers school and was offered a scholarship to St. Mary's in Moraga. Thank God I didn't take that because they dropped football the next year. Things worked out pretty well going to Kansas.

Kansas
I played in '48, '49, and '50. 1947 was my freshman year, but freshman were not eligible. We couldn't even play freshman ball. We were The Big 6 in '47, The Big 7 in '48, and The Big 8 in '50. We grew, but at the same time, that whole time, we were called Oklahoma and the seven doors. We finished second to Oklahoma once and third to Oklahoma twice.

NFL Draft
The draft was not anywhere as big as it is now. The Kansas City Star had a sports editor who was definitely anti professional. He thought the professionals were the big fat guys with the big fat cigars in the back room. When the draft came, there was a small piece added in a box on the sports page that said area boys drafted. John Kadlec, Ed Stephens, and I were the only ones drafted from Missouri. I really didn't know anything about being drafted. About six weeks later, one of the assistant coaches came to see me while I was coaching at Kansas. He wanted to sign me then. Pro football was not what it is today.

I was drafted by the New York Yanks and then I was inducted into the service. I went into the Korean conflict. While I was gone, the New York franchise moved to Dallas, but I never played in Dallas. Then Dallas folded. They became a ward of the league and then they became the Baltimore Colts in '53. I was traded from Baltimore to Cleveland in '53. While I was in the service, I heard the Cleveland—Detroit game on Armed Forces Radio. It was the game where Detroit came from behind and beat Cleveland. I had just been notified that I was Cleveland's property at that time, so I took interest in that game. Then a year later I was out of the service and joined the Browns and we won a world title.

15 Player Trade
Don Shula and I still laugh about how he went from Cleveland to Baltimore. Five Colts were traded, it was Tom Catlin, Don Colo, Herschell Forester, John Petitbon, and me. We all played for the Browns. Only three of the ten players that went from Cleveland to Baltimore played for Baltimore. They were Bert Rechichar, Don Shula, and Art Spinney.

Art Donovan
Art Donovan and I were teammates. In fact, three of us were single, Art, Don Colo, and me. They called us the big three and we kind of hung around together. Art Donovan, of course, he was the son of a famous fight referee. We would go to his folk's home and have dinner.

Paul Brown, Vince Lombardi, & George Allen
I've been associated with three, in my mind, three great coaches: Paul Brown, Vince Lombardi, and George Allen. All three of them were entirely different. Paul was a teacher, he taught us everything every year for the nine years I was in training camp there. We would start off with our stance, how to drive off the stance, and the steps to take. In my mind, he was a great teacher. Vince Lombardi was a driver. He made you think. He worked you so hard he made you think you were better than the other team. And then of course, George Allen relied on experienced veterans, the old timers. He wasn't much of a teacher. All three of those coaches were successful.

Otto Graham
Otto Graham came back in '55. He had made Paul a promise that if they needed him he would come back one more year. So in training camp, we were 0 and 6 and Otto joined us. We won the title in '55 as we did in '54. He was a great athlete. He was also quite the tennis player and golfer, almost a scratch golfer. Plus, he could throw the ball extremely well and he was a great teammate.

Switch from Defensive Line to Offensive Line
Well, you have to go back almost to New York. The New York Yanks were owned by Kate Smith and Dan Topping before they gave it up. So during that season we wound up starting with 32 players and we wound up with 23 because they hadn't made any money for five years. They sold the club to the Miller brothers, but the Millers weren't going to add any more players than necessary. I wound up playing seven games, as a linebacker and an offensive tackle. That's how many players were cut. I had played both ways in college. When I joined the Brown's, Bill Willis, another Hall of Famer, retired and Paul asked me to play the middle line. That amounted to middle linebacker, nose tackle but I would drop out a lot of times in pass coverage. I enjoyed playing defense. In fact, I played defense on goal line situations for quite a few years.

Paul Brown
Paul was one who was not very complimentary. You did your job and he respected you for that, but he never gave much praise. We were playing the Philadelphia Eagles in '54, ahead six to nothing and late in the game they got the ball on the three-yard line. The only time that Paul singled me out, I made a tackle for a one-yard loss on first down. I made a tackle for a one yard loss on second down. Third down came up and the offense was nervous and jumped offside. So it was fourth and seven and then I knocked down a pass. It was one where I dropped out as a linebacker, and knocked down a pass in the end zone and we won the game six to nothing. Paul always gave me credit for winning the game, and having him give me credit in front of the whole team, was the highlight of my career with Cleveland. Stealing the ball from Bobby Layne was good, but that was just one play and I didn't get many accolades from Paul.

Bobby was a notorious rounder. You can go any place and when you start talking about Bobby Lane, they're going to have stories about him.

Radio Helmet
Paul Brown had the first radio helmet and I don't know whether it was banned. He rotated guards and he tried to use a radio helmet. We tried it in the Rubber Bowl in Akron, Ohio. George Ratterman was the quarterback at that time, and all of a sudden he gets a perplexed look on

his face and he looks over at Brown and calls time out. Then he goes over and tells Paul, "Paul, I'm getting directions for cabs to go pick up somebody." They've got the wrong channels." That ended the radio helmet at that time. That was in 1956.

Jim Brown
Jim Brown reported to training camp. He was 6 foot 3 and 230 pounds. He had a 32 inch waist, and thighs about 21 inches in circumference. What a physical specimen, he was just a great athlete and could run fast and strong. It didn't take long before everyone was impressed with Jim Brown.

Bobby Mitchell
When Bobby Mitchell was traded to Washington, they put him at the right position as a flanker. He was a heck of a running back and a great compliment to Jim Brown. Jim was a quality running back for the Browns at that time. Bob was a fine compliment to him.

Len Dawson
The Browns were going to draft Lenny Dawson, but instead, they drafted Jimmy Brown. Later on when the Steelers cut Lenny, the Browns picked him up and signed him. Then Paul cut him, but I don't know why because Lenny was a fine player.

Chuck Noll
Chuck Noll was another one who played offense. He played right guard when I played right tackle and then he went on to be a linebacker later on in his career. We used to call Chuck, Newton because he was smart. Anything he wanted to talk about, he spoke about with authority.

Lou Groza
Lou is something else. We had quite a few Hall of Famers, but Lou was my mentor. He played left tackle and he was just the grand old man of the Browns. He just took care of every young guy.

Gino Marchetti
Gino Marchetti was my nemesis. I go back to the time I was singled out earlier in that Philadelphia game. We played the Colts in Cleveland, and after the game Gino had a field day. He really played well. Paul Brown

looked at me and said, "Michael, I hope your parents didn't see the game you played the other day; they would really be embarrassed." A few years later we played the Colts and I had a good day against him. Of course, we had Jimmy Brown by that time, and we featured the running game as the pass. Gino was the best pass rusher I think I have ever seen.

Decision to Retire
I went to training camp and there was no maternity leave for players. So I was in training camp when my wife had our first girl. We had two boys and another girl. They were all born in the summer, so I told her when she got pregnant again, I wouldn't leave. I just decided it was time.

Joining Seattle Seahawks Front Office
Well, yes it was quite an experience and I credit the Nordstrom's for that because I felt sure I could do the football end of it but they made me President and General Manager. I was worried about all the business details and things like that, but they said that based on their store experience they wanted store managers rather than one of their merchandisers to run their stores. They wanted a football guy to run their football team. I was pleased they had that much confidence in me, and things just went well. They were fortunate to hire a great coach in Chuck Knox, and the rest is history.

First Coaching Job
I went into coaching when Otto took a coaching job. Otto asked me to join him because I had been coaching in the east—west area in the College All-Star Game with him and we hit it off as far as being former teammates in Athens. So when he asked me to join him with the Washington Redskins I didn't think a thing about it.

Joining Carolina Panthers Front Office
Jerry Richardson said he would like to talk to department heads in Seattle because Seattle was the last expansion franchise prior to 1995. I said fine and so Jerry spent about three days with us and then he left and thanked me, of course. Then the new Seattle ownership fired me, they said I was too much like the Nordstrom's so they let me go. Jerry called and he said, Mike, I want to thank you for allowing me to come and visit with all your department heads, and this and that. He said, "I came back and told my partners that we were going to go for the expansion team,

but the only problem was I knew the guy I wanted to run it, but he already had a job." He said, "You don't have one now, will you come down?" So I was out of work that year for two weeks and then I joined the Carolina Panthers. Between Jerry, Mark, his son, and me, we got the franchise and expanded it. That was, the most fun I'd ever had because we hired the whole organization. We built the stadium, dealt with state legislators, and the league offices. It was quite an experience. I really enjoyed it. It's just sad that it came so late in my life.

I'm tickled with this and the fact that we went to the championship game in our second year. We lost to Green Bay up there, but it was really a great experience and a lot of good young kids made that franchise and made it a better franchise.

Pro Football Hall of Fame Induction
The induction is a stage and you think about so many things that happened in your lifetime. There are so many people that had a piece of it. I think we had to deal with it ourselves when we were there. We had a coach that came over and he was a basketball coach and he was supposed to coach all sports. I'll never forget him saying, "Mikey, I don't know a damn thing about football, but I can make you run and I can make you a better athlete, if you would do my basketball drills."

I can remember skipping rope and doing things like that. My senior year they hired someone else who was a good football coach. He came in and I think he perfected whatever I became as far as a football player. It was my senior year that got me scholarship offers and as they say, the rest is history. I was thinking of those people and so many that helped me along the way at the induction.

Best Player Ever
I would say Jim Brown was the best athlete I ever saw. The best play, gee there were so many, you know when you play that long. I would have to go with of all the players that I've played with and again Jim Brown. The best lineman would be definitely Gino Marchetti.

Photograph copyright Associated Press

Chapter 12

Frank Gifford

> College:
> Southern California
>
> Career History:
> New York Giants (1952–1964)
>
> 1977 Inductee Pro Football Hall of Fame

College At USC
We were in the early days of television and everything I did early on was filmed in black and white. It was vastly different.

These days athletes play under a microscope, not only the way they play but the way they live. It's a totally different world.

NFL Draft
I was kind of surprised. I didn't even know that they were drafting that day. I got a phone call from Braven Dyer, a sports writer for the L.A. Times, and he said, "What do you think about going to New York?" I said, "Well I had a great time." He said, "No, you've been drafted by the Giants." I said, "I don't play baseball."

I was only half-kidding because I didn't even know they had a professional team quite honestly. I mean pro football wasn't that big and I wasn't planning to play professionally. I had a pretty good career going. I was doing a lot of stunt work, studying acting, and I was under contract at Warner Brothers at the time. I got married as a senior and I thought, well I'll just go and play football for one season, check out New York, and see the Statue of Liberty and the big buildings. That was back in 1952 and I'm still here.

Acting Career
I did a lot of stunt work. John Wayne was actually a football player at USC. A lot of times USC was able to recruit players by getting them in as screen extras by the screen actor's guilds. On our days off or on our vacation, we would get jobs. They were making a lot of military movies after the war, so there was a big demand for soldiers as extras. It was a good way to supplement our income, which wasn't very much. I enjoyed it and started getting seriously involved studying acting. At one time I was under contract with Warner Brothers. They gave me an ultimatum a few years later. I had to pick football or acting. That year I was the MVP in the NFL. My coach said, "Here's what we will do, don't worry about your contract with them, we'll take care of that, you come and be with us."

Position Change in NFL
I played both ways at USC. They couldn't figure out what to do with me. My senior year I was strictly on offense and we had a pretty good football team. I had a big year. I made All-Coast, All-American, and I was up for the Heisman. It was all new to me. I'd never been in that kind of limelight before. I got that call from Braven Dyer when I was on my way to go skiing in January of 1952. Getting drafted by New York turned out great for me. I got to know the Mara family. They're still good friends of mine.

Transition from California to New York
It wasn't that big of a deal. New York is a very small town really. It just has a lot of numbers. If you live in Manhattan, it's only a few miles long and half-mile wide or maybe a mile at the most. The people are very warm and friendly, and it has a great, great history that I got deeply involved in. I made so many lifelong friends. I'm really blessed. I can't imagine what might have happened had I gone to some other place. I was blessed and fortunate that it was New York.

1958 NFL Championship Game
Well, if I hadn't fumbled a couple of times it wouldn't have been called the greatest game ever played, it would've been a wipeout. I fumbled one time on the way in to score. We were in scoring territory at that time. Then I fumbled another time out of scoring territory. So, I was a big plus for Baltimore that day.

Johnny Unitas was a legendary NFL quarterback. Think of all the players that played in that particular game. It went down in history as a great football game. It was the first game that ever went into overtime. Of course, we lost in overtime and that was a historic thing in itself. It really defined pro football but more importantly, it was nationally televised. Up until that time, there had been only a few games that were nationally televised. When they got the ratings they were astonished. The ratings were just incredible. Something like 75-80% of the television sets in use in the country had been watching that football game. The West Coast had a lot of viewers because it was televised later. It had a 1 o'clock start. That game had a huge effect on the entire NFL in terms of television broadcasting.

In overtime, we had the first possession. We didn't get the first down, so we decided to punt rather than go for it on fourth down with about a yard to go on our own 35-40 yard line. I always thought we should have gone for it because everyone was exhausted at that point. Johnny Unitas and Raymond Berry teamed up on that memorable drive. They came down the field and it was a great performance. There was no question to me that Johnny was one of the greatest quarterbacks of all time and Raymond Berry was one of the greatest receivers. Alan Ameche wasn't bad either.

We didn't know quite what happened. First of all, we ended up tied. Neither team knew what to do. The officials actually didn't know how to go about it either. They didn't know how much time they would have before they would kick off for the overtime, or if they would flip a coin, or who would receive first. We did flip a coin and our team received first. There was one possession by us and then one possession by them. Ameche scored from the two-yard line and that was that.

I vividly remember that play of 47 power. I carried the ball on third down for about a yard. You can make a big deal out of it because Gino Marchetti broke his leg on that play. There was a big pile up on the line of scrimmage. I was fairly positive, I didn't even look at the yard markers, that I had made the first down. The referee came running in and grabbed the ball. Marchetti was screaming like a panther. His bone was actually coming out of his leg. He was obviously very seriously hurt. They were unpiling everybody and they never bothered to put where they marked the ball. Years later I talked to a couple of the officials that were involved in it and they felt the same way. We didn't get a fair mark on it. I'd been playing football a lot of years at that point and when I turned the corner and turned it up field, I had a good block. I broke it back in to the inside. To this day I think I made the first down. I'm not going to make a big issue out of it and I didn't at the time because it would've looked like sour grapes and I knew they weren't going to change it. I've said it and I've written about it. Whether or not we would've gone in to score or to kick a field goal, I don't know, but at least it would've been a different kind of an outcome.

Art Donovan
Arty is great. Art is a big old pudgy guy. You come up to the line of scrimmage and look over and see those guys like Arty Donovan and Gino Marchetti, they were a great football team. If you think about today, what do we have 32 franchises playing football and 50 man rosters? When I played, there were 12 teams that played and we had 33 man rosters. All the good players were being used. There was nothing that you had to have to fill out a roster. If you go down Baltimore's lineup, several of them who I mentioned previously were unbelievable. I feel the same way about our backfield of Alex Webster and me. We both played in many Pro Bowls. Charlie Conerly, our quarterback, was a great quarterback. We had great personnel. It just wasn't as diluted as it has become over the years.

New York Giants Defense 1958
Tom Landry was a player coach at the time and he went on to become a Hall of Fame coach with the Dallas Cowboys. Sam Huff who was the middle linebacker and Andy Robustelli were just extraordinary guys. It was a memorable game and I think it helped define pro football as having arrived in the eyes of the public.

Jim Lee Howell
I was surprised that Mr. Mara made the big decision to hire Jim Lee Howell. I think he hired Jim Lee Howell, who didn't know much about football, because he was a disciplinarian and he had been in the military. They had a bunch of guys who, I wouldn't want to use the word wild, but they were borderline. There were a lot of returning serviceman and guys that were tough to discipline. Jim Lee Howell could handle these

guys much better than Vince Lombardi. Tom Landry was a player coach. I think that he made the move for those reasons. Of course Lombardi went to Green Bay and put together a Hall of Fame career. Tom went to Dallas and he put together a Hall of Fame career there.

Decision to Retire
My head hurt and I didn't want to hang around like a lot of other guys. More than that, I started working in 1958, my last season, in local television doing local news. I did network radio with Phil Rizzuto, and I knew what I was going to do. I had a place to go. A lot of guys at that time, like I said, had returned from the military. When they left football they didn't really know what they were going to do. I knew what I was going to do and I couldn't wait to do it.

I played 12 years. That was long enough. There was a change in coaches. Allie Sherman replaced Jim Lee Howell and that was a disaster. Not personally, but he arrived with the football team just coming apart. Guys were retiring, guys didn't like him, and I knew when it was time to get out.

Chuck Bednarik
I keep trying to tell people that I had a spinal concussion. They didn't have the CAT scan in the 1960s when I got the famous hit by Chuck Bednarik and was lying on my back in the field. Years later, I start getting a lot of numbness and tingling in my arms. By then, the CAT scan was available and I went to see a specialist. The technician who did the scan asked me what year I was in an automobile accident. Bednarik wasn't a car, but I had multiple fractures of the vertebra in my neck. It's a good thing I decided to take a year off because had I gone back and tried to play it may have been much worse than it was. Taking that year allowed everything to heal. People remember me for only as getting hit at that point, but I came back and played four more years and I went to the Pro Bowl again as a wide receiver. That injury didn't define my career, it was just a dramatic thing that people kept replaying over the years. In fact, I think it was on a postage stamp in Philadelphia.

Favorite Position to Play
I just loved to play. I played as a defensive back and I doubled up a couple of times as an offensive back too. I was a tailback in the single

wing when I came out of USC. I made All-American as a tailback. I could run and I could pass, I could block and I could catch. For several years I was the leading receiver and the leading rusher with the Giants. I just loved to play football. I don't think that I could've had the career that I had if I was playing today. Everything is so specialized today. I just loved to play.

Don Meredith
Don Meredith was a wonderful friend. He really was. He was an incredible guy. We got to know each other on Monday Night Football and we stayed friends after that. He was one of a kind. His life was far too short.

Kyle Rote
Kyle Rote could've done anything he wanted to do. He was a dreamer. He was an artist. He was a remarkable person. He would've been an unbelievable football player. He was fantastic at SMU and one of the people that inspired me to go in to professional football. I happened to be listing to the radio when Kyle and SMU were playing Notre Dame. It was the most fascinating radio call I'd ever heard. He was drafted number one by the Giants; the year before I was drafted number one and he got hurt that season in training camp. They were going to play me on defense and so that was the reason I went over to the offense. Kyle had torn his knee up and never did recover from that. He limped through a pretty long career with the Giants and he made the Pro Bowl a couple of times. God only knows what he would've been had he not torn that knee up before his first football game.

Howard Cosell
Howard Cosell told us he was a lawyer. I wouldn't want him representing me. Bless his heart; he's gone on to that great gridiron.

He was okay. He really was. He had a great mind. His name was really Howard Colon and at the time he felt that there was a great prejudice against him coming into the broadcasting world. He was defensive about everything and Lord knows he might have been right about a lot of things at that point of time. He could be very difficult but there were things that he was brilliant at. He had a remarkable memory. He had a way of interviewing that few people did. It was more of an interrogation.

He arguably was one of the first people, at least in radio and television, who wasn't kissing up to somebody when they interviewed them. Howard asked the questions that other people wanted to know the answers to. He was one of the first people to do it. Now they all do it.

Being a Traffic Cop in the Booth Between Howard Cosell & Don Meredith

Well, at times but I never felt that way. I've heard that over the years. Don like I said was one of my dearest friends and we lost a real beauty in him. He didn't miss much; I can tell you that on the way out.

Monday Night Football

I don't think that there is destination television any more unless there is a moon launch or something like that. There's just too much out there. Everything seems so focused now. There's nothing that crosses over the demographics and reaches out to an entire country like Monday Night Football did. A lot of people tuned in to watch it because they had never heard anyone like Howard Cosell. A lot of them wanted to see what Don Meredith was going to do to punch through that balloon, that arrogant guy that was on TV. They didn't even know what football was about. Some people tuned in to watch the game itself. There was so much that surrounded it. There will never be a circumstance like that again because everything is covered night and the day. It's just a world of difference. I said many times, we had the best of times, we really did.

New York Giant Y.A. Tittle passes a snowball to teammate Frank Gifford. Photograph copyright Associated Press

Chapter 13

Yale Lary

> College:
> Texas A&M
>
> Career History:
> Detroit Lions (1952-1964)
>
> 1979 Inductee Pro Football Hall of Fame

College Choice
First of all, Texas A&M scouted me in high school. I had several offers, the Naval Academy, Notre Dame, University of Texas, A&M, TCU. I chose Texas A&M.

Jim Brown
I played against Jim Brown for several years. He made a classic statement about me. We played him in championship games and beat him every time. He said, "Well, I never did know if Yale was going to block me or tackle me." He gave me a nice compliment. He's very friendly, and we've remained friends for a long time.

Texas A&M
It was just a military school, so to speak. It was an all-boys school, when I went there. They had a lot of returnees from World War II. I went down there in 1948, and graduated from there. I'm glad I did. I got my commission down there and went during the Korean War. I served for two years. That took two years out of my professional career, but I came back alive. That's the most important thing.

NFL Draft
At the time, professional football wasn't very popular in Texas. They got to see the Thanksgiving game with Green Bay and Detroit. I wanted the challenge. I was honored that Detroit drafted me as high as they did. I was their first draft choice they kept. That's quite an honor to be their first pick. I was very flattered for the choice that they made. They made it for a pretty good reason, I guess, because I had a fabulous career up there.

I went up there just to make some money. I was just married and needed to have a job. I could have had a job when I graduated from A&M, but didn't want to. I could have been a coach in high school or maybe college, I don't know. I was thrilled to death to make the team.

Bobby Layne
Bobby Layne was the best. His famous saying was he never lost a game. He just ran out of time. I believe that. He was by all means the greatest.

He was a competitor. He pitched at University of Texas and never lost a game. I don't think he lost any football games either; not very many. He was just a great competitor. He was naturally talented.

Buddy Parker
Buddy Parker kept to himself. When he said something to you, you better pay attention because he didn't speak too much. He was very worried about everything including the team and the individuals. He was a fabulous coach. He won a lot of games and championships.

How he Became a Punter
During World War II, I was at a military football game. I was in junior high school, 12 or 13 years old. Army was playing another branch of the armed services at a high school football stadium. When the football was kicked for the extra point, it went over the fence and I caught the ball. I started punting it in the street. It just came natural.

Jack Christiansen & Jim David
We played together quite well. Instinctively, we knew what one was going to cover; if he could or couldn't cover. We just worked together and played together well.

NFL Championships
It was wonderful, a real thrill to the team. Of all the teams, you're the best team up there and that's saying quite a bit. It's quite an honor. Especially when you didn't have all those teams. It was quite a thrill. We won the world championship three times in '52, '53, '57.

Buddy Parker Quitting & George Wilson Taking Over as Head Coach
We didn't believe it when we went to the 'Meet the Line' banquet in downtown Detroit. Buddy Parker got up and said that he quit. That was a real shocker to us. What can you do? George Wilson was a good coach.

Joe Schmidt
Naturally, he was a great ballplayer and just a tremendous leader. He could get everybody together and raise their spirits. Joe Schmidt was an inspiration.

Doak Walker
Doak Walker was just a wonderful man. He was always nice. He could do everything: run, pass, kick field goals, and extra points. I always wanted to be like him. I could do a few things like him, but not many.

Favorite Moment in the NFL
I guess winning the world championships was my favorite NFL moment. That's what you're there for. I just wanted to make my family proud of me—my lovely wife and my two children. Of course, I was pleased with my performance and was thrilled to receive the honors I got.

His Speed
I was pretty fast. In high school, I was ten flat. They never timed me in the professional ranks. I was fast enough to return a few kickoffs or a few punts. I had some good moves, and I was fast. Doak Walker wasn't really fast either, but he had the ability to find that little gap. I did too on several of them.

Bobby Layne
I don't think there's any question that the stories about Bobby Layne were magnified. He was a real good friend of mine. A lot of writers have

to write about these popular individuals and they picked him. He was very outspoken and didn't hide his activities. He was a great ballplayer who was noticed for every win.

Dick "Night Train" Lane
Dick "Night Train" Lane had to replace Jim David. When Jim David retired we needed somebody over there and Lane was available. He was a great defensive back. It's hard out there. Your all by yourself and you're a cornerback and spread in that way, and there's a receiver out there, one-on-one. He was a good one.

Pro Football Hall of Fame Induction
I didn't expect it or plan on it. I was very honored, of course. I started to feel like I deserved it when I looked back on my career.

Toughest Quarterback
Johnny Unitas was probably one of the toughest ones. Norm Van Brocklin was really tough too. None of them were easy.

Favorite Player Growing Up
My favorite player was my dad. He played football at the same high school I did, North Side High School. I didn't have a favorite college player. I was too busy playing high school ball. I played every sport there was in high school.

I made all conference in baseball for Texas A&M. We went to the World Series. I made a home run in the World Series and we beat Ohio State 3 to 2. Marty Karow coached me at A&M and then he went to Ohio State. It kind of gave me a thrill to hit a home run against him in Omaha.

Paul Hornung Naming You The Best Punter in NFL History
That's flattering. We didn't have the domes like they have now and all that stuff. We had to play in ice, sleet, snow, and rain. The elements weren't favorable. I feel like I did the best I could do at the moment. I'm proud of what I did.
Career

I played in Detroit with Doak Walker, who is one of my favorites and was one of my very good friends. I knew Sammy Baugh, of course. I played against him one year before he retired in Washington.

Retirement from NFL
I was offered several opportunities to fly over to Detroit on the weekends and punt, but I declined. There's no question that I could have played a lot more. I could have played defensive back, I thought for a couple of more years. I could have punted for no telling how long.

Photograph copyright Associated Press

Chapter 14

Bob St. Clair

> College:
> University of San Francisco & Tulsa
>
> Career History:
> San Francisco 49ers (1953–1963)
>
> 1990 Inductee Pro Football Hall of Fame

College Choice
There were other colleges I could have gone to, but I was married at the time and the University of San Francisco was giving me a housing allowance to live off campus instead of living on campus. It was home and we were raising a family. At that time we had one child, and my wife was pregnant. A lot of the guys who were from out of the area or weren't married would live in the old barracks they had on campus. I would get the equivalent of the value of that. It wasn't very much, but it was something.

College Team
We thought we were pretty good once we started winning and beating other teams. We had a lot of confidence. We had a great coach, Joe Kuharich, who later coached for the Redskins. There are three of us in the Pro Football Hall of Fame, Gino Marchetti, Ollie Matson, and me. There's a fourth in the Hall of Fame who was from our class, our publicist, Pete Rozelle.

Coach Kuharich had two cement posts that were wrapped in canvas and cushioned. It was enough for just one person to get through. We'd get in a three-point stance on each side and he'd hike the ball. We battled our way through using our hands. It was almost like a fistfight.

Ollie Matson
The interesting thing is he was such an offensive threat, yet he made All-American on defense his last year 1951. Isn't that something?
He played both offense and defense. We all did in those days.

Burt Toler
When Pete Rozelle became the Commissioner, he made Burl Toler the first black NFL referee. I remember going out on the field and I'd come out behind Burl and hug him. He turned and looked at me the first couple times and said "No, you can't do that. You can't do that."

1951 University of San Francisco Football Team
I think man for man we could have beat anybody. I really do. We never really had a chance. No one would play us. The year before, we had played Stanford and Cal and they had beaten us. We almost beat Cal that year. They went to the Rose Bowl in 1950. So in 1951 we thought we'd be able to play them again. No way. They didn't want any part of us. It had nothing to do with having black players on the team. Not here on the coast. It was just that they felt that we were that good and it's a no-win situation for them. They were supposed to beat us, and if they lost it would be really a black eye to them.

1951 Orange Bowl Not Allowing Black Players from University of San Francisco to Play
We were going to play Georgia Tech in the Orange Bowl but when we got the invitation the coach said, "Well, what do you guys want to do? Do you want to have a meeting?" We said, "We don't even have to have a meeting, Coach. We're not going to go for this. This is crazy. We're not doing this."

We didn't care what color they were. What the hell? That was a slap in our face. Obviously they wanted us to lose, we thought. Evidently the Bowl Committee, and this was very prevalent in those days had that kind of attitude. In fact, I think one of our officials was told that this is very common in the south at all the bowls. They don't accept black players.

They're making a movie about our team. Gino and I are going to be in it. I have already filmed some parts of it in San Francisco at Kezar Stadium where they named the field after me. They filmed the old locker room and some nostalgic stuff. I played 189 games there.

Bob St. Clair Field at Kezar Stadium
It was a real honor to have the field named after me. I mean, usually you have to be dead before they name anything after you. I looked in the mirror the next morning after the naming and said, "Geez, do I look that bad?"

Transfer to Tulsa University
I went to Tulsa University my last year because that was the only team that would recognize a transferee. USF had dropped football because they couldn't afford to field a team anymore after we refused to play in the game. There would have been enough funding to last for a few years if we played in that game. What happened was I went back to Tulsa University. They would recognize me as a transferee without having to sit out a year. That is what I was interested in and I played the year back there.

NFL Draft
I was finished at Tulsa when I was drafted by the 49ers. I received a call from the owner, Tony Morabito and he said, "Bob, we are so happy to have you, a local kid, playing. You went to Poly Technic High School, University of San Francisco and now with the 49ers." He said, "You're a perfect fit here. We're going to give you a little more money than we do the average rookie. We're going to give you $5,500." I said, "Well, I'm sorry, Mr. Morabito, I can't accept that."

The only reason I said that was because the guard drafted next to me had just signed a contract with Green Bay for $6,000. So, I thought that was the figure and I didn't want to look like a piker. He hung up the phone. I had to wait a week back in Tulsa before he called me back. He said, "Listen, St. Clair, you better be as good as you think you are. We're going to give you the extra $500."

Diet
I eat raw meat. Even today I eat raw meat. I don't cook red meat at all. In fact, I'll go in a restaurant and order a rare chicken and they'll look at me and have me sign a release. Ever since I was a little kid I can

remember my grandmother in San Francisco chopping meat at the chopping block in the kitchen. When she was chopping up meat, the dog and I would be looking up at her waiting for her to throw a piece of meat. She'd give me or the dog a piece. I'd always be fighting that damn dog trying to get as much as I could away from him. I just acquired a taste for raw meat. The thing is, my favorite food is raw liver. I still like it today. You can't get it in a restaurant but I'll buy it at the store or a butcher shop. Every once in a while I really enjoy that.

I can remember when the rookies first came into camp when I was playing. I was the captain of the team and on Thursday night we would have liver at training camp. I would get my raw liver, put a napkin over it, and walk over to where the rookies sat. Most of the rookies sat by themselves in training camp. I'd sit with them and I could see the expressions on their faces.

They'd look at me and think, "What the hell is the captain sitting with us for? Jiminy Cricket." Then I'd take the napkin off and there'd be blood all over the plate, and I'd start chewing on the liver. Most people don't know raw liver tastes and sounds like an apple; it crunches. I'd exaggerate it naturally and let a little blood drip down my chin. All of those guys would get the hell away from me. They would get up and leave, saying, "I'm not as hungry as I thought I was."

Nickname the Geek
There was a movie that came out when I was playing called Nightmare Alley, with Tyrone Power. He was called the Geek in the movie. His character was part of a circus side-show and ate live chickens. They would throw him a live chicken and he would rip it apart and blood and feathers would be everywhere. That is where I got my nickname. A guy said of me, "That's the Geek" and it stuck.

Y.A. Tittle
I thought I'd died and gone to heaven when I was drafted by the 49ers and I came back to my hometown. I had gone to high school in San Francisco, I played at the University of San Francisco, and then with the 49ers. The day I went to training camp Y. A. Tittle was assigned as my roommate. I thought it couldn't get any better until I slept in the same room with him for a couple of nights. He's an asthmatic and he wheezes

at night. No one wanted to be his roommate because they couldn't sleep very well. I had to come up with a plan because the training team told me I looked a little sleepy. They wanted me to make the team.

The next night the coach, Buck Shaw, came down and was talking with Y.A. about the next days practice. He said, "Practice tomorrow at eight o'clock." As he was leaving the room he said, "I'll turn out the lights." I said, "No coach, let me."

We had beds on the opposite side of the room and there was a little sink. I got up and I played like I was getting a drink of water. I said, "I'm going to get a drink of water."

I faked it and then I turned out the lights. Then I turned the corner went to Y.A.'s bed. I reached under the covers and kissed him on his bald head. Then I patted him on his ass, and whispered in his ear, "Goodnight, Y." He never slept a wink all night. He told the whole team I was gay.

San Francisco 49ers Y.A. Tittle, left, Hugh McElhenney, right, and Bob St. Clair in the middle. Photograph copyright Associated Press

Chapter 15

Joe Schmidt

> College:
> Pittsburgh
>
> Career History:
> Detroit Lions (1953–1965)
> As Coach:
> Detroit Lions (1967–1972)
>
> 1973 Inductee Pro Football Hall of Fame

<u>NFL Draft</u>
I was disappointed, not from the standpoint of coming to Detroit, but I didn't really think I had much of a chance to make a championship team. They just won a championship the year before. I really wanted to play for the Pittsburgh Steelers. They had told me through the grapevine that they were going to draft me. So I was planning on being a Pittsburgh Steeler. I came from Pittsburgh. That is where I went to school.

I was excited about the possibility of being a Pittsburgh Steeler. As I listened to the draft on the radio the rounds went by and eventually the Lions drafted me. I thought I'd go up there, give it a shot, and see what happened. Everything turned out for the best. I played on some great teams and with some great football players. I have had an extremely exciting life here in Detroit.

I had an older brother who played for the Steelers. He played at Carnegie Tech in Pittsburgh. He played for one year before he had to go into the service. I always felt that's where I belonged. I was anxious to play professional football, naturally, and especially in my hometown.

If you take the point where the Allegheny and Monongahela Rivers join the Ohio River and you go down the Ohio River, and you take a radius of about 30 miles within that point, you have some great football players. Joe Montana and Johnny Unitas lived about a mile and a half from where I grew up. Then there was Mike Ditka, Tony Dorsett, and Dan Marino, Jim Kelly who played for Buffalo, and of course Big Joe Namath. There are quite a few Hall of Famers within that area. I would say there are probably 10 to 15 guys from Pittsburgh, Pennsylvania that are in the NFL Hall of Fame.

Running Backs Who Gave Us The Most Trouble
I don't know who gave us the most trouble. Probably the running backs that we played against gave us the most trouble. There is a whole list of guys including Jim Brown. We played the Browns quite frequently. I always looked at Rick Casares as a great football player from the Bears. The 49ers had Hugh McElhenny and Joe Perry. During that time most of the 12 teams had pretty good running backs. At least one of whom who was pretty damn good. The guys I mentioned always gave everybody trouble.

Bobby Layne
Bobby Layne gets credit for a lot of things that really never transpired. There are all kinds of stories about him. I don't want to paint him as a choirboy or anything of that nature but he liked to go out and have a good time. When he stepped on the football field in practice and in the game he was all business. He enjoyed himself. He would always drag a couple guys around with him to a few places. That was his mentality.

In spite of that he was always prepared to play. He always knew what he had to do. He always played up to expectations. Like everybody else he had bad games, naturally. He set the pace for everybody. He wanted everybody to play to the maximum. I know of a couple times during the course of his career where somebody wasn't blocking properly on the offensive line and he would stop the game and go over and tell Coach Buddy Parker, "Get so and so the hell out of the game. He's not playing."

Of course at that particular time we only had 33 guys on the team. So we didn't have the luxury of taking some guy out and putting another guy in. He said, "If he keeps it up and he doesn't start blocking, I am coming the hell out. I am not playing." He expected everybody to perform properly.

Alex Karras
Alex Karras was quiet. He wasn't much of a practice player. He was a game player and was a good player. In my opinion he should be in the Hall of Fame. Being that he had some problems there with gambling and so forth, I think that is the thing keeping him out of the Hall of Fame. Alex had very quick hands and quick feet and he was very strong. When he played I don't think there were too many guys who could block him.

Radio Headsets
Radio headsets were new to football. The receiver was in my helmet and my defensive coach would call the plays. A lot of times he would take his time. The offensive team would be coming up to the line of scrimmage and I had to get the defense set. So I would call it and he would get a little upset.

He had to do his job and I had to do my job. If the play wasn't in on time, I had to do what I thought was best. We got in a few contests about that. It was something they were experimenting with. I would prefer to call my own defenses. He felt that it was necessary for him to be involved with it. So I had to go along with it.

Transition from Player to Coach
It was difficult to tell you the truth. I was only on the staff for six months prior to becoming head coach. One year I was a player and the next year I was a coach. Everybody I coached, or everybody on the teams I played with, were good teammates and good friends. Coaching friends at times was difficult. I had to make some adjustments and cut some teammates. We had rookies coming in and I had to replace my former teammates. It was difficult from that standpoint. Everybody was watching me, naturally, at all times. So it was a little touch-and-go at times, but I think we were able to handle it. It got a little tight at times. Of course when you are coaching everything doesn't go properly. So you have to make adjustments accordingly.

Chuck Hughes Death During Game

Unfortunately at that time, physicals and things of that nature were not adequate. They didn't do the extensive testing that they do today. Chuck Hughes whole family had congenital heart problems. That wasn't really established when he was getting a physical. Of course, he kept it quiet.

The game was against the Bears. He wasn't a starter but he was always walking next to me asking for me to put him in. We were losing in Tiger Stadium against the Bears and I put him in.

It was the end of the game. I got him a pass and he ran down the field. It was like a long pass pattern. He came back and then he ran another one. Then he came back and he dropped down. He died right there on the field. It was quite an experience, for the whole team, the whole organization, and of course, his family. It was difficult to move on.

I still think about that every football season and I think about his family. It is difficult to erase that from your mind. It was an unfortunate thing. I guess these things happen in life. That naturally put a damper on our season that year. The whole team flew down and went to the services in his hometown in Texas.

It is difficult to get the team back to thinking about the game when something that drastic happens. We didn't have anything like grief counseling. It was hard to get over. I don't like to use that as an excuse for our season, but it affected us.

Photograph copyright Associated Press

Chapter 16

Raymond Berry

> College:
> Southern Methodist
>
> Career History:
> As Player:
> Baltimore Colts (1955–1967)
> As Coach:
> Dallas Cowboys (OE) (1968–1969)
> New England Patriots (1984–1989)
> Detroit Lions (QB) (1991–1992)
> Denver Broncos (QB) (1992)
>
> 1973 Inductee Pro Football Hall of Fame

<u>High School</u>
I wasn't big enough or good enough to play in high school. By the time I was a senior there wasn't anyone else there, so I got a starting position at 150 pounds. I was about 5'10 in those days, but I had a size 12 foot. My nickname in high school was skis. There wasn't any snow in Paris, Texas either.

<u>College Positions</u>
My junior and senior years I was the left end and we ran the Straight-T Formation, with no split receivers whatsoever. We went both ways, playing offense and defense.

I was the left defensive end, which in today's terminology would be an outside linebacker. I was on the end of the line, but I played in the three-point stance most of the time. Forrest Gregg and I played side by side for two years together. We played both offense and defense in those days. We didn't throw the ball any, we just ran the ball from a Straight-T Formation and played good defense. I loved to play defense. I was a natural defensive player. That was what I liked to do. I didn't know anything about being a receiver. I didn't get introduced to the passing game until I got into pro football with Baltimore.

College
I caught 33 passes in two years, my junior year and my senior years. We just didn't throw much at all. We ran the ball and played defense.

Draft
I'll put it this way. If Baltimore thought I was a future Hall of Famer they certainly underpaid me. I made $10,000 in my first two years and I was one of the higher paid guys.

As a matter of fact, I was a 20th round draft pick. That was the year they drafted 30 players. They took me on the 20th round after I finished my fourth year in college. I was a junior college transfer so I actually went five years to college and my junior year at SMU was my fourth year in college, I was eligible for the draft so they drafted me in the 30th round. They drafted me to play offense.

Baltimore Colts
It wasn't fun whatsoever. I was expecting to get cut at any time. The only thing that saved me and actually, it's the only reason why I ever got to play in the NFL is I happened to arrive in Baltimore at the right time, at the right place, with the right people. I happened to arrive in Baltimore when they had no veteran receivers. I arrived in Baltimore when that team had only been in existence for one year. They had no veteran group and they had no veteran receivers.

My rookie year there was 13 rookies that made the team out of a 33 man roster. I couldn't have made it anywhere else I would have gone in the league. They didn't have anybody so I got to play. I got to be a starter and I played 12 games. I ended up catching a tremendous number of passes. I caught 13 passes in 12 games. That was my production. I didn't know my butt from first base about running pass routes, about getting away from man to man coverage. I didn't know anything about the passing game and how to get open or anything. I did have a natural pair of hands and I could catch and I could run and jump. I was 185 pounds that was my credentials.

Johnny Unitas

If you had seen Johnny Unitas and me in training camp in 1956, you may have gone away sobbing. We were two pitiful cases of football players. Fortunately, we had a coach named Weeb Ewbank who saw something nobody else did. He saw something that we didn't know anything about and I'm glad he did.

John made the team as a backup quarterback. That was 1956, Johnny's and my second year. Johnny was cut by the Steelers the year before. He made the team as a free agent quarterback because we needed a backup to George Shaw. George Shaw was a number one draft pick who played my rookie year. I think he was rookie of the year in the NFL. He was a great athlete. He got a severe knee injury around midseason of that year.

We were playing the Chicago Bears in Chicago and George got a severe injury. Unitas came in and he threw a touchdown pass on his first completed pass. The touchdown went to the Chicago Bears though. That was his first completed NFL pass. A defensive corner out there for Chicago, who probably got a raise in salary in the following offseason picked it off. If you had been a close observer that day, you may have picked up something that nobody, I don't think, really recognized. That was John a free agent trying to hang on in the NFL, who never gets to play, finally gets to play, throws a touchdown pass to the Bears on his first play and then the rest of the game, he just goes about his business like nothing ever happened.

What you were getting was insight into this guy's mental toughness, competitiveness, and confidence. He had it in spades. That was a real tipoff, because it didn't faze him a bit. He went about, had a very decent day, and the Chicago Bears ended up being world champions that year.

When I came back for my second year, I was due to be replaced. They had drafted two All Americans for my position when I came to camp. It was just a matter of time before they were going to give me a bus ticket out of town. I didn't have anything in my life but football. It was the most important thing in my life and I loved to play. My world was getting ready to end. Johnny Unitas came as a free agent. He'd already been cut the year before and he loved to play football. He didn't have anything else on his mind but that.

We were two highly motivated players who loved to play, wanted to play and didn't want to leave. One of the things that you need to understand is that in this highly organized day of modern football, I don't know how many coaches even allow time for players to work on their own after practice. Every place I coached after I left the game as a player and started coaching, the head coaches got so carried away with what they're doing that they didn't allow any time for a receiver and quarterback to go out there and work on their own.

A lot of coaches don't even want them working on their own. They're afraid something will be out of their control so they don't encourage it. Instead, coaches discourage it and just don't allow it. Weeb Ewbank was totally the opposite. He had learned under Paul Brown with the Cleveland Browns. Paul Brown always allowed his receivers and quarterbacks to spend as much time on the field on their own after practice as they wanted. Weeb saw great results from that, those great Cleveland Browns passing games of the Paul Brown era.

He encouraged it, allowed it and gave us a time to do it. We stayed out there as long as we wanted to. We worked and got to know each other. We developed timing that you just couldn't get any other way. I realized there is a confidence factor involved in this. Something clicks in the quarterback's head when he works with a receiver on that type of the basis for a long period of time. He gets to the point where he just knows that receiver, he knows when he's going to break, he knows the timing of his plays and he has great communication with him and great confidence.

In the heat of the game, I think without question, the quarterback will invariably go to the receiver he knows is going to be where he's supposed to be, when he's supposed to be there. I think that's exactly what happened with Unitas. We worked as one. We were a unit. I know in games Unitas was given the responsibility of calling plays. Weeb

Ewbank recognized an instinctive play caller in Unitas. He let John call the plays.

I wasn't old enough or mature enough to understand, but Unitas would call on me on some plays because he knew I was going to be where I was supposed to be and he knew I was going to catch it.

Art Donovan

Art Donovan is a totally different case. He couldn't do anything, but eat and play football. He could play football well and he certainly could eat. He couldn't run, but he didn't have to. Playing defensive tackle if he could just take three steps one way or the other that's all he needed.

Lenny Moore

The result of Lenny Moore's work after practice with Johnny Unitas ended up exactly the same as it was with me. I think that this type of after work practice, was one of the reasons we won two World Championships in Baltimore. Look at the games we played against the New York Giants defense, which was the leading defense in the league. Key plays were plays we had perfected, talked about, and worked on after practice until they were automatic. In the heat of the game, those things just came up and happened. It wasn't an accident. That after practice work with the quarterback allowed us to gain confidence with him. That was the key to our success.

Frank Gifford & 1958 NFL Championship Game

I've heard Frank Gifford talk about bad spots in the 1958 NFL Championship Game. I think he really believes that. I looked at the film very closely and I really disagree with him. I don't think the official missed the spot of the ball at all. I think Frank hit the ground and bounced. I think where Frank bounced to was not where the spot of the ball should be put, but actually when you hit the ground that's where the ball should be spotted. The bounce doesn't count after that. I don't think any of us realized the significance of the game. I don't think we were old enough to understand at all. I don't think we had a clue. I think we were just thrilled to death that we were able to win the game and be part of the history and the significance of it. I'm not saying that nobody understood it. I think there were some people that did. I think the man that really understood it and this came to me years later as I began to piece together the chain of events was Bert Bell.

I think the man that really understood the significance of that game immediately was Bert Bell, the Commissioner of the League. I saw him after the game. I can't remember exactly what the circumstances were, but I saw him face to face, very shortly after that game was over. The memory of his face that day will be with me forever. Bert Bell had tears in his eyes and he was crying. I saw his face and then went on about my business, but that picture of him with tears in his eyes stayed with me. Years later I'm beginning to put it together. Bert Bell understood that this league, that he had been nursing for several years and doing everything he could to bring it to prominence, he knew that his baby was born.

The rulebook had been structured. Someone realized that in a championship game, they had to have some policy for a tie game. I don't know who came up with the rule, but it was in the rulebook. Of course, nothing like that had ever happened. Nobody even knew about it.

The head referee in that game was a veteran referee and he knew the rule. I remember being out on the field when that game ended in a tie. We all thought the game was over. We went to our benches thinking it was a tie game. We didn't know anything about overtime. Nobody had ever talked about it. That official came over to the bench and explained to Coach Ewbank the procedure. That's when we realized we were going to keep playing.

I don't know if any of us realized the significance of sudden death. All we knew was that we were going to keep playing. We went out on the field and when we got the ball, we went about our business without realizing the significance of what was happening. I know that the Giants won the toss and got the ball, but our defense stopped them. They punted and we were 80 yards out. We knew this was no longer going to be a tie game. We weren't fighting the clock anymore. We were 80 yards out and it's a 17-17 game.

Unitas comes in the huddle and he just methodically starts mixing run and pass. He moves the darn football 80 yards and when we get into field-goal range, a lot of people later on had this big question why didn't you kick the field goal? I was out there on the field with Unitas watching him, I was under his spell without even realizing it. Weeb Ewbank had given Unitas authority, the free rein to call the game. In this particular situation, the last thing on his mind was getting a field goal. He's going to put that ball in the end zone. He just mixed run and pass. I think it was 13 different plays, five or six passes, seven or eight runs, and move it all the way in. Alan Ameche went in for the final three or four or five yards to score. As soon as that happened, the game was over and we all turned and started running toward the clubhouse. There wasn't any extra point. The official explained the first team that scores, wins. Ameche scores, the game is over 23-17.

I didn't realize at the time, but without question, that game was the greatest game that I ever played. As I said, I wasn't doing anything. We had a very basic, simple offense. I had about four or five pass plays and that was all we had. We weren't doing anything complicated. This simplicity was the genius of Weeb Ewbank.

He made the decision about how many plays he was going with and that's all he did. I played under him and we used to beat a bunch of teams because we could execute. That was Weeb Ewbank's philosophy. He had very few plays, but we knew how to run them. Over the years I've came to realize that it takes a genius to keep it simple.

Pickup Game In Central Park Against Giants
As an assistant coach I kept working out and running in Central Park for several years.

When we got the word that they wanted to reenact the game in Central Park, I was still able to run pretty darn good. The Giants weren't the only team that was five or six years older than when we had played them in '58.

All the players were getting older. Out there on the field that day, I could run darn near full speed. John Unitas and I, hadn't been on the field together in about six years.

We started running those routes and it was like there hadn't been any break. I was telling him this is how I can get open on and he'd call it. We'd run it and complete it. It was a replay of the earlier game in a way. It was very interesting to me that this several year gap happens, and Johnny Unitas and I stepped onto the field that afternoon and he was putting the ball right on the money. We were like when we were playing. You would have never figured that could be the case.

His Phenomenal Hands
This is how it works. First of all, I think you're born with it. I think it's a physical gift at birth. I think it has something to do with heredity. For example, my dad was only 5'8 and probably weighed about 155 pounds, but he had big hands and big feet. I ended up being 6'2 and 185, and I got big hands and I got them from my dad. From the time I started playing football, I could catch the football without even thinking. It was just a natural gift.

When I got to the professional level and was catching the fastballs at the speed with which Johnny Unitas was throwing, I found that I was dropping footballs that I should have been catching. Very early in my years with Unitas, I started practicing catching like I'd never done before. I really studied catching all the different type of catches. I ended up with a list of 12 different situations in the short ball, and six different situations in the long ball. There are 18 different drills. You've got lowball, highball, behind you, too far left, too far right etc. I just started drilling and I would catch 60-70 balls. I'd go right down that list catching three or four of each type.

It was drill and repetition. It's the exact same thing you do when you take a typing course in high school. At first, you don't know anything about typing. Your hands have never been on a typewriter, but you complete an exercise that you go through every day. Drill and repetition, drill and repetition and by the time the semester is over, you know how to type and you'll never forget it. I see the same parallel in catching. If you perform catching drills like catching the high one over your left shoulder over and over, then more than likely in a game, you'll catch the high one over your left shoulder.

His Footwork
There were a couple of things that helped me with my footwork. I ran track every year I was in college for five years. I worked with the sprinters, doing whatever they did. I developed speed and quickness during those years. Of course, there was a lot of heavy speed work I did over and over to get faster. At some point, I developed these drills for footwork. I would backpedal and backpedaled fast. Then I'd be backpedaling and I would twist to my left and go three or four steps, crossing over. Then I'd twist to my right and crossing over.

I had a whole routine of quickness drills that I developed. I did those on a regular basis, especially in the offseason. I did them over and over. There's no question my speed began to increase because I was still growing physically. When I went into professional football I was still growing. Two years after I started playing professional football, I probably finally leveled off.

During the first two years I played, I spent the off seasons working out. I worked out February through July, when we started training again.

I was running and doing all these agility and quickness drills, but I couldn't find anybody to throw to me so I had a hard time working on catching. I had the footwork, the quickness, and the speed. I was getting such a high level of conditioning and strength that I hardly ever got injured. I went through most of my pro career without even getting hurt.

Pro Football Hall of Fame Induction
I was coaching, I believe I was at the University of Arkansas in 1973, when I got word about it. It was the first year I was eligible for the Pro Football Hall of Fame. I wasn't surprised. In my sixth or seventh year in the league, I broke the NFL record for receptions and then broke the record for yardage. When I retired as a player, I held the record for the most passes caught in a career. I think I had the most yardage gained through receiving in a career. So when the time came, I knew pretty well I was going to be put in the Pro Football Hall of Fame. I wasn't really surprised.

Toughest Defensive Backs

There were five or six tough defensive backs that were the toughest. I played 13 years so I came up against some great ones. Right off the top of my head, there was Abe Woodson of the 49ers. By the way, two of the four or five I'm going to name were 100-yard dash sprint champions in the Big 10.

Abe Woodson came from Illinois. I think he won the 100-yard dash in the Big 10 track. He had tremendous speed. When he came to the 49ers, they put him over in the corner. I faced him twice a year, at least five years in a row. He tried to cover me conventionally for a while. He really introduced the bump and run on me. He walked up on me. The first time he did it, he just got right in front of me like a yard off.

He didn't understand though that he was not keeping me from getting inside on him. The first time he did it, we just completed a bunch of passes inside. The second game of that season then he walked up there on me and he got inside of me. He was going to cut me off from getting inside. That puzzled me for a few quarters. I couldn't figure out exactly what I should do because the guy could run. He was right up on me and I didn't know what to do.

Eventually what I realized was we had to beat him deep. That's what we had to do every time he walked up there. I'd give him three or four moves in the first five yards. Then, we timed a deep pass that I could catch fading away toward the boundary. He had a hard time covering that one, but I couldn't get anything short on him so we just had to go deep.

Irv Cross was the next guy I think about. Irv brought a whole different problem to me because that guy was big. Abe Woodson only weighed about 175 pounds. Irv Cross weighed about 195, and had won the 100-yard dash in the Big Ten. He tried to cover me conventionally the first time or two I played and I ate him alive. He walked up on me and started taking me on at the line of scrimmage. He gave me a fit trying to get away from him. When we had the collision, I lost it and then I tried to outrun him. He won the race. For a couple games there, I had one heck of a time trying to figure out how in the world to get open on this guy.

Dick Lynch of the New York Giants was another one that he was very smart and he studied you, but he also crowded you. He came up and he crowded you and he'd take you on early. You just couldn't run conditional patterns on him. He knew what he was doing and he could run. He wasn't real big either so when collisions came, I didn't walk away with anything worse than a tie and sometimes I'd win the collision. With Irv Cross, I couldn't win the collision.

Jesse Whittenton of the Green Bay Packers came along with Lombardi's teams. He was tough to get away from because he was another guy who would line up five or six yards deep, but he only backpedal a yard and he'd just walked squat. When you got down there, he was sitting there waiting on you. He took away all your conventional stuff. It took me a while to figure out how to beat Jesse. Going deep on a guy like that was the thing we did. John and I were pretty good at timing a deep ball so we did have something against him. Those four guys were very challenging.

Coaching
I'll tell you the formula for coaching is enjoying coaching first and foremost. If you get great players, you enjoy coaching.

When I inherited the New England Patriots job, I'd been out of coaching over two years. I was living in Boston and working. I had a friend there that had a business and he had hired me and I was working for him. I was making a living outside of coaching. I wasn't even thinking about ever getting back in it again. I had been fired too many times. I was tired of it.
The Patriots fired Ron Meyer right in the middle of the season. That was 1984. I get this phone call. Understand, I've been out of coaching now for two, two and a half years. I'm making a living. I'm personally happy. I know enough about the coaching profession, and no I ain't missing it. Pat Sullivan gives me a call and says, I'd like to come over and talk to you. He came over at the house and talked and he said, "We're going to fire Ron Meyer." They had six games left on their schedule that year. He said, "I'm offering you the job."

I said, "Pat, I'll call you in the morning, with my decision about it." I thought about it long and hard because if you had been in the coaching business long enough you knew the drill. I was tired of getting fired and moving. I thought about it and I thought I think I need to do this. I gave him a call and said, I'm coming over. I'm coming to work. I drove over there and walked in as the new Head Coach of the New England Patriots with eight games left on their schedule. I hadn't been in coaching for two and a half years. I didn't know anybody on the coaching staff except maybe one guy. It was Ron Meyers' staff.

I knew about six veteran players on the team, all the rest of them were new ones that had been brought in since I had been let go two years prior. This is a Thursday and we have a game against the Jets coming up on Sunday there in New England.

That's how I got back in the coaching business. I didn't have anything to do with it. I started looking at this football team and trying to get familiar with the players. Everywhere I looked was talent and depth. I thought to myself this football team has got everything you need to make a run for a championship. They got depth. They have two quarterbacks, Steve Grogan and Tony Eason both of them you could win with. With a 16 game schedule in the NFL, you better have two quarterbacks because trying to get one of them through a season healthy is a major accomplishment.

We had four great wide receivers and two fine tight ends. We had an offense line that was as good as anybody could hope to have and depth there. Then on defense, we had four great corners that could cover anybody man to man, three great safeties and a slew of linebackers and we had good defensive linemen. This team was loaded. I thought to myself what have I inherited here? This team can run with horses. That's the team that I inherited with eight games left. I started learning and getting familiar with the personnel. I think that during that eight game stretch we won four and lost four if I remember right.

<u>Super Bowl XX</u>
By the off-season, I realized what we had. When the season ended, I told all the coaching staff, all of whom had been brought there by Ron Meyer, I told all of them. I said, I'm going to hire my own coaching staff now. I said, "Any of you guys can apply for the job and I will hire some of you." "When it's all over and done with, you're going to be on my

staff." There was about two or three of them that did apply and I kept them. There was two or three of them that left.

The good part about it was I knew this team was ready to win if we could just keep it simple. The biggest problem you got with taking over a new team is the learning process that a team's got to go through to learn the system. You just can't operate at full physical ability when you're trying to learn and you're in learning mode. The first year a lot of times is not productive because you just can't go on all cylinders.

The special teams coach I kept so we didn't have to change the special teams system. The defensive coordinator was Rod Rust and I kept him so we didn't have to change our defensive system. Their offensive system was not good enough to win in the NFL and I knew it after I took a look at it. I hired a new offensive staff and in the off-season we installed a new offense. When training camp came, our biggest problem was on offense and it showed up in our early games. I think that after six or eight games, we were playing five hundred football, but then they began it to get it. We got on a roll and won eight or nine in a row to get to the Super Bowl.

When we went to the Super Bowl, we had a first year offense and it was A, B, C. I'm not real sure if it was even C, but it was A and B. It was that simple and that basic. The theory was and it wasn't just a theory because I'd been around long enough to know that if you've got great players, don't confuse them, let the physical abilities flow. If you put too much on their minds, it ain't going to work. I knew I had great players. I didn't want to screw them up. It went A and B and it did us well all to the Super Bowl.

The problem with an A and B offense when you come up against a PhD defense, you've got a problem. We couldn't score against the Chicago Bears. They had a defense they had been putting together for five years. They had a defensive minded coach over there named Buddy Ryan that was as good as it got in the NFL. They had a great defense with great personnel and a great defensive scheme. Our little A, B deep offense just was not up to handling a PhD defense so we couldn't score and got our butts beat.

Best Defenses Of All-Time

There's no question about Buddy Ryan's defense. All you have to do is look up the numbers. Looking at the NFL since the '50s, I would rank the Chicago Bear defense in 1985, in the top four or five that I've ever seen. When ranking the Pittsburgh Steelers, I'd look at the defenses under Chuck Noll. They had a great defensive coach up there, Bud Carson. I would say that was the best defense I've ever seen.

I would put Tom Landry's Dallas Cowboy defenses in that ranking too. George Allen with the Washington Redskins was a defensive genius. He was with the Chicago Bears when they won the World Championship. Then he went on to be a head coach. Playing against George Allen's defense was a full day's work. Those are four or five of the best. Buddy Ryan is as good as any of them.

George Allen

You had your work cut out for you when you were playing George Allen's teams when he was with the Bears, Rams, or Redskins. He was an absolute defensive genius. No question about it. Buddy Ryan's defensive scheme was right there with him. I'll add Tom Landry, Bud Carson, and Chuck Noll to that group also.

I had the privilege of facing all of those guys. I was with Forrest Gregg and the Cleveland Browns for two years. One year, we had to play the Steelers twice. I saw them up close and personal for two years. They had personnel and a scheme; it was just a great defense. If you want to have a nightmare as a receiver, just go up against Mel Blount all day.

Best Player All Time

Jim Brown and Johnny Unitas were the best. They are in a class all by themselves. Jim should have been outlawed. He was something.

We played in Baltimore in 1959, and won the World Championship that year. We played Cleveland in Baltimore another year and Jim Brown scored five touchdowns. They beat us 35-28.

Photograph copyright Associated Press

Chapter 17

Forrest Gregg

> College:
> Southern Methodist
>
> Career History:
> Green Bay Packers (1956–1970)
> Dallas Cowboys (1971)
>
> As Coach:
> San Diego Chargers (1972–1973) (Off. Line)
> Cleveland Browns (1974) (Off. Line)
> Cleveland Browns (1975–1977)
> Toronto Argonauts (1979)
> Cincinnati Bengals (1980–1983)
> Green Bay Packers (1984–1987)
> SMU Mustangs (1989–1990)
> Shreveport Pirates (1994–1995)
>
> 1977 Inductee Pro Football Hall of Fame

College Choice
SMU was in the Southwest conference and they were probably as good as Texas at that time. My high school football coach went to SMU and he encouraged me to go. He felt I would like it there.

I played both ways. I played what we called inside tackle on both lines. I did a lot of pulling and double-teaming. I played all sports in high school. I played basketball, baseball, and was on the track team.

NFL Draft

I was drafted in the second round by the Packers in 1956. I wasn't sure where Green Bay was. I had to get the address and then check. I thought it was up in Minnesota or somewhere like that, or Illinois. I didn't know. I found out quick where they were. The Packers weren't very good around that time.

Early Years with Packers

It was a change because a lot more pass blocking was required. It was great. There were a lot of outstanding football players. Competition was fierce.

When I got to Green Bay they weren't sure where they were going to play me. They didn't know whether they were going to play me on offense or defense. I got to play a little bit of defense during training camp. We opened with the Bears that year. The Bears beat us. I think I played about three plays on defense and I played on special teams.

I really wanted to play defense. I thought I could play defensive end.

I was drafted in '56 and went into the Army. I was in the Army in '57 and missed one full season and one game. I first met Willie Davis when we played football together at Fort Carson, Colorado. He got out of the Army before I did. He went back to the Cleveland Browns and was traded to Green Bay the next year.

Green Bay had a terrible season in '58. That was the year before Lombardi came. We were 1-10-1.

Vince Lombardi

After the '58 season was over, I went back home to Dallas and got a job. I also finished school. I needed three credit hours to finish my degree. When I went back to school, I got a job working with the school. I heard that they had fired Scooter McLean who was the Head Coach and hired some guy named Vince Lombardi, an assistant coach from the New York Giants. I didn't know anything about him.

I went to some SMU sports functions in downtown Dallas in the spring of '59. I ran into a friend of mine named Donnie Goss. Donnie had played for the Cleveland Browns and was traded to the New York Giants. Donnie asked me, "You know anything about that Lombardi that they hired in Green Bay?" I said, "No I don't Donnie. Do you know anything about him?" He said, "Yes, he's a real bastard." That was my first knowledge of Vince Lombardi.

I went to training camp and didn't unpack my bags right away because I didn't know if I was leaving. Lombardi turned out to be the greatest coach of all time. He was a disciplinarian. As Henry Jordan said one time, "He treats us all the same. Like dogs."

He was tough but fair. He treated everybody the same. It didn't matter who you were. Bart Starr, Paul Hornung, or some other player, were all treated the same. If you didn't perform up to his expectations you heard about it. I think one of the things that made him great, was he expected to win. He had great expectations of every player. You thought, if Lombardi thinks that I'm good enough to do this, I must be. That's the kind of guy he was. He was a good football coach, a knowledgeable coach. We had a physical team. He expected us to win.

We had a challenging football team. That was basically the thing; you look back, not necessarily at the starting positions, but at the team. It was basically the same team that went 1-10-1. The talent was there. What needed to happen was we needed to be put together. Like I said, he had great expectations of us and would not accept less.

Not one player ever got away with anything as far as breaking the rules were concerned. You just didn't get away with it. If you missed meetings, you were fined. If you were late for a meeting, you were fined. If you were late for curfew and you were caught, you were fined.

Paul Hornung
Paul Hornung respected Vince Lombardi. Paul was great football player. He was a team player.

Vince Lombardi Calling Forrest Gregg The Best Player He Ever Coached

I can't even begin to tell you how I felt. Of all the great players that he coached in Green Bay, New York, and Washington; for him to say I was the best player he ever coached made me feel very humble.

Favorite Moment in NFL

I think probably one of the biggest games we ever played was the '61 NFL Championship game against the Giants. We had a pretty good high school team but we never won our district. We never got into the playoffs. When I was at SMU we had a lot of fine football players. We never got into the playoffs or went to a bowl game.

I remember going out onto Lambeau Field in 1961. Jerry Kramer had been hurt earlier in the season. They moved me from right tackle where I'd made All-Pro, to right guard taking Jerry's place while he was hurt. I remember being introduced and running out on the field for that game. It was an awesome feeling. We were able to score pretty well that day and we beat the Giants. At that time it was called the World Championship.

Super Bowl I

The big thing about Super Bowl I was the uncertainty of the competition that we were playing against. We met some of those guys playing for the Kansas City Chiefs coming out of college, but there were a lot of them we didn't know. The only thing you could tell about them was their size. We would watch them play against teams who we didn't know anything about. We didn't know how good our competition was. Going into that game, we were picked to win. We were representing the old guard, the National Football League. We were expected to win. We were able to pull it off and that was awesome.

I never saw as much media in my life as we saw during that week prior to the game. We went to Santa Barbara, California and worked out. We were playing the game in the Coliseum. We had the media following us all week long. There were television and newspaper reporters, the Associated Press, radio, you name it, they were there.

Chicago Bears vs. Green Bay Packers Rivalry
It was never like any other game playing the Bears. Vince Lombardi wanted to beat George Halas but he wanted to beat everybody.

As far as the Bear's defensive linemen, the one I remember most of all was Ed O'Bradovich. Ed and I banged heads together usually three times year; because it seemed to me, we always played the Bears in preseason and twice during the regular season. Ed and I competed against each other. We were both about the same age. He was one of my favorite players. He wasn't a dirty football player but he was a tough football player.

Comparing Ray Nitschke, Bill George, & Dick Butkus
Ray Nitschke said he was the better player. He was my teammate and I'd have to agree with him. Dick Butkus said he was better and Bill George said he was better. Don't ask me to pick because they're all great football players. It was fun playing against them because I knew I was playing against the best. One way to measure yourself is how you stand up against the other guy when you're playing against the best.

Year with Dallas Cowboys
That was a great year for me. Dallas had been to the Super Bowl the year before I got there. After I had retired from Green Bay, I moved to Dallas and was selling sporting goods. Dallas had a bunch of offensive lineman get hurt during training camp. Tom Landry called me and asked if I would be interested in playing. I remember getting my football shoes and reporting to their training quarters, which was north of my home in Dallas. I went in the locker room with my football shoes in my hand, and those guys looked at me like, what in the world is this guy doing here.

On the way to my locker, I ran into Herb Adderley who I played with at Green Bay. We got to talk. Then I ran into Bob Lilly. We knew each other well and he was a welcome site to see. Knowing that you've got great players like those guys on your team, makes you think, we have a chance to win, and we did.

Tom Landry was a great football coach. Tom was one of the most knowledgeable football coaches I ever had. Offense or defense, he knew the p's and q's of both sides of the ball. He was a good teacher and the system that he used was a lot like the system in Green Bay. Lombardi had been the offensive coordinator with the New York Giants and Tom had been the defensive coordinator. They both adopted that Giants way of doing things. That wasn't totally strange to me except the Dallas offense was much more complicated than Green Bay's.

Coaching Career
I always wanted to coach. I had a job opportunity in sporting goods. It was a way to making a good living. I always thought in the back of my mind that I would like to coach. I guess one of the things that; I said, Well I can't be Vince Lombardi. I'm not like him. If that what it takes to win in football, I don't know whether I can do that or not? Then to go out and play for a guy like Tom Landry, who was similar in a lot of ways to Vince but not the disciplinarian. Tom had expectations of his players also. I think that's one thing that I think they both learned from Jim Lee Howell in New York. There was a lot of peer pressure with the Cowboys. I guess that's the best way to describe it. If you were the starter you were expected to perform with a winning attitude and a winning performance. I never was a starter there but I noticed the players. If you didn't perform well in a game, some guy beat you and sacked the quarterback, you're teammates looked down their nose at you. I would say that was one of the differences in Lombardi and Landry.

I thought I can't be like Vince Lombardi and win because you've got to be yourself. I thought there's Tom Landry who was exactly the opposite as Vince Lombardi and he won, so he was himself. He wasn't' anybody else and didn't try to be anybody else. That's the same way it was with Vince.

I thought well if that's the case then maybe I've got a chance to win as a coach. That's what put me in the direction of coaching. I knew after that season that I probably wouldn't play anymore or maybe shouldn't play anymore. I started looking for a coaching job when that season was over. I got an offer for a line coaching job at San Diego.

Raymond Berry

Raymond Berry and I played side-by-side in college. I played left tackle, he played left end. He was also at that time playing both ways. Raymond was a smart ball player. He looked at the other people's offense and figured out what they were trying to do. He also did that on the other side of the ball. I never had to worry about a player getting around the corner before I would have a chance to make a tackle. That was good for the team and good for me. Raymond was a tough and physical football player. He grew up in a football home. His father was a high school coach in Paris, Texas and had been there most of Raymond's life. Raymond grew up in a football family. He also had great hands.

Pro Football Hall of Fame Induction

I never felt that I would be in the football Hall of Fame. I strived to be the best that I could be. I wanted to win football games for Vince Lombardi. I thought about the Hall of Fame but I didn't know whether it would ever happen or not. There are very few people that make it. I just don't know what the numbers are right now. Last time I counted there's not a lot of players inducted into the Pro-Football Hall of Fame. It's just a dream come true.

Ed O'Bradovich

Recently I have been diagnosed with Parkinson's disease. One of the nicest letters I ever received was from a guy named Ed O'Bradovich who wrote me a letter and gave me a lot of encouragement in fighting this disease. There are some things in your life that you'll never forget. I won't forget that letter that I got from Ed and the encouraging words that he gave me. I just think that he's a big old guy, he was a tough football player, and played every down to the best of his ability.

Photograph copyright Associated Press

Chapter 18

Lenny Moore

> College:
> Penn State
>
> Career History:
> Baltimore Colts (1956–1967)
>
> 1975 Inductee Pro Football Hall of Fame

<u>College Choice</u>
I wasn't really thinking about college. My brothers enlisted in the service and I thought I'd do the same. They enlisted in the service because that was one less mouth to feed at home. They would get allotment checks and send them home to help out with expenses. I didn't see anything down the road. I just took it year by year. My high school coach, Andy Stopper, stayed after me and encouraged me to go away to school.

Next thing you know, it was my senior year of high school and colleges were calling me. Thank God, as I said before, for Andy Stopper. He said, "Lenny, you've got to go away to school. You need that college education."

Then prayerfully he said, "You'll do well with the football team. I'm not concerned about the football side because I know that you're going to be all right there. So I'm going to stay after you and hope that you go away to school."

The high school line coach was a guy named Bob Perugini. Bob Perugini went to Penn State, and that's when the door opened up for me. We just kept it right in line, and that's where I ended up.

Rip Engle
Rip Engle was my college coach. Bob Perugini and Andy Stopper, opened up the gates for me at Penn State.

Joe Paterno learned from Rip Engle. That I know. In fact, Joe had even said before his death, that he learned what he knew from Rip Engle. Both of them were at Brown University. Rip Engle was the head coach at Brown University, and Joe Paterno was his quarterback. Joe was all set to go to law school. When Rip took the Penn State job, he brought Joe with him. That's how Joe ended up at Penn State. They had a father-son type of relationship. Rip just kept Joe under his wing. Joe learned Rip's disciplines and coaching style. He tried to keep the same thing going when he became head coach in the '60s, after Rip retired.

Penn State in the Mid-'50s
For men of color at Penn State, which was predominantly a white university, there were some things that were very difficult to deal with because there were certain places I couldn't go. Aside from that, there was no place to get a haircut. We had to learn where we could go and where we couldn't go, and what we could do and what we couldn't do. A lot of our time was spent in the dorms, I'll put it that way.

Baltimore
The same racial issues were everywhere and very difficult to deal with. When I got to Baltimore, black athletes basically had only one area to go for entertainment, and that was Pennsylvania Avenue. Pennsylvania Avenue was just about the only street that was wide open to us, where we could seek entertainment and places to eat, without going through the race process.

I checked with a lot of the older guys like Ollie Matson, Marion Motley, and Buddy Young. Those guys were there way before me. I'd ask them how they dealt with things, especially when I went out of town. You couldn't go anywhere if your hotel was downtown. You couldn't go to the movies, you couldn't go in certain stores, and things like that.

That was pretty common in most of the major cities. You just had to deal with it. You were confined to the hotel. There were a few places we stayed on the outskirts of town. That way the team could stay together without splitting up. That was typical all over the league.

We also knew that number of black players allowed on certain teams was going to be limited. We talked to each other about situations; how it was going and how we were dealing with it. It was always keep your mouth shut, do what they tell you to do, and just be cool.

I thank God like I said, with the atmosphere, the separation of blacks and whites, you never knew what was going to happen down the road. You just didn't know. You couldn't just relax and think, everything is okay, because it wasn't okay. It was about being careful and watching yourself, because you didn't know what was going on. We would check with the other guys of color on the other teams. They were going through the same things.

It wasn't until years later that you heard that every team was given a quota of how many black athletes could be on a team. You weren't able to go over that number. Of course, we didn't know that. We always did the best we could and prayed that we became a part of the team. That was the way it was.

Baltimore Colts Teammates
It was about whatever God-given abilities we had, that Raymond Berry had, and that John Unitas had. That really encompassed the team because we knew, regardless of what the situation was, once the game was over, they went their way, we went our way. You know what I mean. That's just the way it was during that time, but we knew that we had to come together as one and play to the best of our abilities. There was no separation on the team, just business as usual.

I played against Alan Ameche in college when he was at Wisconsin. I didn't know anything about Raymond Berry until we played for the Baltimore Colts. I realized that collectively, we grew together as one team. That was very, very encouraging because we knew we needed each other. We also knew that for us to move ahead, we had to give the best we had, whatever our abilities were. For me, it was a lot of praying. I did a lot of praying and hoping that everything was going to work out for the best.

I knew nothing about Johnny Unitas. I knew nothing about any of them, with the exception of Ameche. All I knew about him came from when I played against him. As far as their backgrounds and things of that nature, I knew nothing about them at all.

We had to work as a team, but once the whistle blew, they went their way, we went our way. That was unfortunate because we didn't get a chance to really know each other during those early years.

Spats Nickname
When I was in college, Rip Engle's Penn State team was what you would probably call Plain Janes. They had plain uniforms, plain everything. Just simplicity. No dressing up, so to speak. The backfield guys couldn't wear low-cut shoes. If you looked at other teams, most of those backfield guys wore low-cuts. Rip's backfield guys had high-tops, just like the linemen. Everybody was dressed the same. Rip Engle wanted everybody to be the same.

Bob was a backfield guy who had hurt his ankle. Of course, with the high-top shoes and stuff, he had to get his ankles really taped up. I just strapped myself down with high-tops. Of course, they made comments. What are you doing with that tape on your shoes? I said, "Well, it makes me feel good", as I taped it on the outside. It did make me feel good. I just kept doing it.

Now what I did was, as they would tape the guy's ankles, there was always a little bit of tape left on the roll that they would throw in the trash. So they couldn't get on me about using tape. I would maybe grab about a half a dozen of those rolls and tape my shoes.

Of course, that became a fixture with me, even when I got in the pros. I did the same thing. I said, "I'm not wearing low-cut shoes. I'm wearing high-tops." A lot of the backfield guys looked at me and said, "Man, what are you wearing them old shoes for?" That's what I did. It's just something I learned in college and I just kept it going.

Johnny Unitas
Fortunately for me, I had the opportunity to go to quite a few Pro Bowls where they always had the top quarterbacks. I was able to see some of

the top quarterbacks in the league and compare them to Johnny Unitas. I said, Man, Johnny is better than these guys, or at least he's as good as, if not better than, a lot of these guys. He just didn't get the publicity or have that kind of publicity until we grew as a team. Going into our second year, we got into the playoffs. Then of course '58 we were world champions, and '59. The rest is history as far as Johnny U was concerned.

He was a guy that, whatever ability he had, he used it and took it to a different level. He pushed himself. Johnny was his own man. He learned. He watched a lot of film, which is the key to really knowing the game from the inside out. Not only that, he had the great Raymond Berry with him. Both of them watched films like crazy. Nobody else on the team really watched films other than when we had our meetings, because when practice was over, boom, everybody hit the locker room, and we were on our way home. That's the way it was.

Raymond Berry
Raymond Berry came to me, and I never ever forgot it and said, "Lenny, I've been watching films. Based upon what I have seen from the films we need more of you in our offense." I was wondering, what in the heck is he talking about. I said, "Weeb Eubank is our coach. He's the one that calls the shots. He's the one that gets us in position." He said, "You can catch, so why can't we use you a little bit more often as a wide receiver?"

We started working on pass patterns and running pass patterns and he told me, "You're going against the great Dick Night Train Lane!" I'm looking right at Raymond the whole time. He said, "Night Train Lane knocks the hell out of people. He's one of them guys, he will throw that form at you and you've got to learn to get away from him. But in the meantime, he's giving himself up, Lenny. There are certain patterns I've got that we can do against a guy like Night Train. That's how I ended up being a wide receiver as well as being a running back. Running back was something I always did.
Also, fortunately for me, I went both ways in college. In college, I was a defensive back as well as being a running back. Now, at Penn State, we didn't throw the ball that much, but at least I learned how to tackle. I learned how to cover, as a defensive back would do. I learned how to

bring punts and kickoffs back and that kind of thing. I was a good special teams man because I did it all the way through college.

Coming into the pros, putting me in other positions wasn't a handicap for me. It wasn't hard for me to make the adjustment. Thanks to Raymond Berry, who was the one that came up with the idea to use more of me in the wide receiving position. This opened it up for him as he was the wide out on the other side of the field. That's how all of that happened.

He told me, "Lenny, John is not going to throw the ball to you unless you work with him." What that meant was to stay after practice and work with Johnny on running pass patterns to get the timing down. Raymond said "Johnny's got to have the confidence that he knows where you're going to be and how you're going to cut on certain patterns. Never cut on your inside foot, because you'll be out of balance. Make sure that you cut on your outside foot if you're going to make a sideline cut. Make sure your outside foot is your plant foot." "

He was so right, because when I started practicing these patterns and things like that, I understood exactly what he was talking about, to get the body in sync so that you would have your hand-and-eye coordination together. All that came from Raymond. He worked with me on running pass patterns and things of that nature. That's how I learned.

The drill that most pro teams use today, was started by Johnny Unitas in 1958. They called it the "two-minute drill." Nobody did that but Johnny U, and that was back in 1958. That was something that we worked on just for the 1958 NFL Championship, because nobody did any kind of a two-minute drill. You'd get right up to the line of scrimmage and he call the plays right up on the line. Other teams didn't do that. Guys would always break out of the huddle and the quarterback would get up and call the plays. We didn't huddle.

<u>1958 NFL Championship</u>
There was confusion when the game was over, because we were tired and nobody knew what to do. The referees and the officials weren't sure what to do. They called their own huddle and were trying to figure out

what to do. They talked to the head coaches, and decided that we needed to play another quarter and try to work it out.

The officials decided that whichever team scored first, won the game. Other than that, they weren't sure exactly what to do. They weren't sure if we should play a complete quarter or end the game once one team scored. They made their decision, and the rest is history. Gino Marchetti got hurt in that game, and they took him off the field in a stretcher.

Art Donovan, Big Daddy Lipscomb, & Roger Brown
It was unusual to see guys that big. Big Daddy was about 280. Donovan was about 275. That was huge for defensive linemen. Most of the defensive linemen were 240, 245, maybe 250, at the most. When you had guys like Donovan and Big Daddy Lipscomb and Big Roger Brown, from the Detroit Lions, weighing about 300 pounds, that was an unusual.

Gino Marchetti
Gino Marchetti was as active as any defensive end could possibly be jumping over people, getting around people, and just lightning fast. He developed the position. Most guys that came after that learned from Gino. That was it, because most of the time, most of the linemen took care of their own territory and then released, but Gino was fast.

You had offensive tackles trying to block Gino. Man, that was a job and a half for them, because there was nothing they could do to hold him up. Gino was that good, that fast, and that strong jumping and getting around.

Pro Football Hall of Fame Induction
The only thing I thought about it was, 'Gosh, what an honor,' when I got in. You had to wait like five years to be eligible. During my third year of eligibility, they said I just missed out, and then I didn't make it the fourth year. I think I got in the fifth year. I think that's the way it happened. But no, it's just a question of getting in. Man, with such a high honor as that, wow.

Is Jim Brown Best Player Ever?
Well, when you say "Best player ever," that's a heavy subject, to say "the best ever." Jim Brown's is in that category. I could probably say that he's one of the best.

Jim Brown was something else. No question about that. When you start mentioning good or top running backs, Jim Brown is right there. Rules have changed over the years and the way things are done, but Jim, no question, is up there among the tops.

Affiliation
Definitely I am an ex-Baltimore, not Indianapolis, I am a Baltimore Colt. I don't support the Indianapolis Colts. I am a Ravens fan to the nth degree. The Ravens are my team.

I was working for the Colts at the time that they left Baltimore, in one of the front-office jobs doing public relations. You could hear the talk going around that Bob Irsay was thinking about moving the team, but nobody really mentioned how serious he was. The next thing you know, boom. Here come the trucks and everything was gone. He was a very, very unusual man, to say the least, in his way of doing things.

We're not Indianapolis Colts. We are Baltimore Colts alumni. That's who we are. When they left, they left. I can't give enough kudos to the fantastic Art Modell. What a tremendous, tremendous gentleman. I grew as I got to know him. He was that grand of an individual. You could see, everything he did was one for all, all for one. Fortunately for us, Carroll Rosenbloom was a great man also.

Baltimore Colt Lenny Moore is met by Detroit Lion defensive end Darrius McCord Photograph copyright Associated Press

Chapter 19

Bart Starr

> College: Alabama
>
> Career History:
> As Player:
> Green Bay Packers (1956–71)
> As Coach:
> Green Bay Packers (1975–83) – Head coach
>
> 1977 Inductee Pro Football Hall of Fame

<u>College Choice</u>
I grew up in Montgomery, Alabama. My Dad was in the military so we lived all over the country. In my final years of high school, he was able to stay in one location for a few years so I was able to stay in the same school.

I met this beautiful lady whom I'd fallen in love with in when I was a senior in high school. I stayed at the University of Alabama because I discovered that she was going to go to Auburn. Originally I was planning to go to Kentucky and play for Coach Bryant. I thought to myself, if I go to Kentucky, and she goes to Alabama, I'm going to lose her. I call it the greatest audible of my life. I chose to go to Tuscaloosa where I could get an old jalopy or something, so I could drive to see her and at least keep that relationship alive. It turned out to be a great decision because I married her.

The University of Alabama is an excellent school and I knew that going in. I really enjoyed it. I was in the business school there. It was just super fun and a great challenge. I enjoyed all four years.

Draft
I didn't know that much about Green Bay. I knew where it was obviously, but I wasn't that familiar with it. It was a joy and an honor and the longer we stayed there the more we came to love it even more. It is a tremendous community. The people are fabulous and I'm not exaggerating. They're as great you'll find anywhere. They were inspired by that low round draft choice. I was going to prove to them that I was worth it. I understood why I was a low round draft choice. At any rate, I'd worked extremely hard. I'd never worked so hard in my life before going to that first Green Bay Packer training camp.

We weren't a powerhouse, but I just wanted to get into the NFL and to play there. The more reading I did about Green Bay, the team franchise, the community, the more I was falling in love with it. I could hardly wait to get up there.

Packer Offense
The way plays were called how they were established and what the rationale was and so forth and so on was a change. That too led to an excitement, a challenge, because it was something a little different than what you had perhaps been associated with somewhere else.

I enjoyed our offense because it was solid. The offense was solid because it was based on the run more than the pass. In those days, we had some very strong runners. Obviously, we were taking advantage of that and we had some excellent offensive linemen.

By having that as a core, our passing game was very effective. We could run play-action passes as though it was going to be a run and pull back and pass and so forth. It offered a great challenge for us and it was a very strong challenge for our opponents.

I didn't know the size of the playbooks that some of the other teams had. We were very strong and very solid. We had everything built around a core of plays. We obviously had excellent alternate plays off of those core plays. What we had that was very strong on Coach Lombardi's part, was the core of an offense that was so sound and so solid that it was unbelievable. We were very, very proud and pleased with it.

Being a Backup in Green Bay

You want to play and you understand why maybe coaches are going with someone else. They have different reasons. They know more about the other person and so on and so forth and they're staying with them. I felt that it was a challenge each day in practice. You wanted to perform better so they would see you as a possibility of working into that starting slot.

Vince Lombardi Hiring

We didn't have any idea at all. We were just interested and reading a lot about him and following him and so forth, but no, we had no idea at all because we had not been exposed to him that much.

It changed immediately because when he held his first meeting with us I could tell within 15 seconds that this man was truly going to be special. The way he approached the meeting, he had about 10 or 12 of us, a mixture of offense and defensive players.

His approach was so solid, so sound, so simple, and direct that you couldn't wait to get to the next little piece he was going to talk about. I'll always remember our first meeting because after we were in it for about 45 minutes we took a break. I ran a short distance down the hallway there in the Packer office building where we were holding the meeting and got on the pay telephone and called my wife back in Alabama. All I said to her was, "Honey, we're going to begin to win."

The championships were not all because of him, but primarily because of him because leadership starts at the top. You have to have strong leaders if you're going to accomplish anything. Obviously you have to have the people with you that form the team. That's what that leader does because he's going to get great assistant coaches, good players and so forth. They build an organization. It was so obvious, as I said, from that first meeting that we were going to change and going to win. That's when I was so pumped.

Losing the first and only championship game he ever did was difficult on him, he moved on immediately after it because that was typical of Coach Lombardi. It was a disappointment so he used that as a plus, as a tool for building, rebuilding and going on and winning the next ones.

Super Bowl I
It was exciting, very challenging, and thrilling. We were just blown away and honored to be in it. Little did the traditional NFL people know how strong that game was and how good the Kansas City Chiefs were because I can tell you unequivocally the Kansas City Chiefs were an outstanding team.

I think that we were very strong as a team because we had been together for longer than they had been. We were able to handle them quite well. I don't think enough people realize how tough every play was. The Chiefs were good and we didn't just run all over them and so forth, and blow them out of the stadium. That was just not the case at all. The Chiefs were very well coached, extremely talented group, and we had a fierce competitive game going on, which we knew going in.

Coach Lombardi had done a great job of preparing us for it. We didn't over look it and didn't just think that this was a secondary kind of league that we were playing. He saw how good the Kansas City Chiefs were.

He was typically a sound and thorough coach. He was extremely well organized. Lombardi was very, very well prepared, and thorough in his approach of handling different people in different positions throughout the team.

Paul Hornung
Paul was quite a gentleman. He was vibrant, alive, and despised curfews. He and Max McGee, I don't know if they ever made two curfews the whole time they played with the Packers. Coach Lombardi fined the heck out of them and went on about his business because he knew how good they were.

Max McGee Super Bowl I
Ironically, I saw Max McGee the morning of the game and knew that he had been out all night. I was going down to pick up a paper the morning of the game. I was walking toward the front desk to pick it up. On my left was one of the entrances of the hotel and walking through, and this was at 7 a.m. the morning of the first Super Bowl is Max McGee. My thought was oh my God, here we are in the biggest, greatest game of our

lives and this guy has been out all night. He had been but you saw what he did. He just played like gangbusters during that ballgame.

Bob Skoronski Not Being Inducted Into Pro Football Hall Of Fame

I can tell you one player that is very, very deserving and I think it is disappointing he is not in. I root for Bob Skoronski each year and write about him each year. He was our offensive captain and our left tackle, blindside tackle, for me. He was a fabulous, fabulous tackle. Flip that over and on the right side was Forrest Gregg. Forrest Gregg went into the Hall of Fame with me in 1977. If you looked at the grades on Monday morning following ballgames the marks for Bob Skoronski and Forrest Gregg were almost identical.

I'm not sure how the selection committee is structured, but I'm obviously very biased. I've seen others who have gone into the Hall of Fame since we went in years ago. With no disrespect to them; many of them are good, but I have yet to see an offensive tackle or lineman go in there that's anywhere close to what Bob Skoronski was.

Most people unfortunately don't have a clue because of all the media that was directed toward Forrest Gregg, and deservedly so. He deserved it. Bob Skoronski also deserves it.

Ice Bowl

We were very confident because the lead play on short yardage in that ballgame was a wedge play, meaning you had two linemen somewhere up front coming together with a wedge against a single defensive player. With no disrespect to anyone we ran the wedge play on one of the defensive players with the Cowboys. We had run it two or three times. We had run it once before we scored and had gained yardage on it then. We knew the play would work. It was very, very strong.

The Cowboys developed a submarine technique where their linemen charged so low you couldn't block them. All you could do was fall on them except for one defensive lineman who was so big and tall he couldn't get down that low. His charge angle was up and you could just knock him back. We'd seen it, we'd done it, and we'd did it out on the field.

Unfortunately, the ground was so slick and so hard it was tough to get footing to make it go. That's why we scored on that play that we called because we got enough footing and got in. Rather than give the ball to the fullback, whom we had used on that play, and him slipping and sliding on the ground that was so hard, I was upright. I could shuffle my feet and then lunge in. That's why we called that play when we did.

Coaching Green Bay
It was very tough and very demanding and a very poor mistake on my part. I don't think that you can get into something and do it successfully unless you prepare well for it. I had not prepared to coach. I had no ambitions to be a coach. I was delighted to be where I was and what I was doing.

I think if you're going to be a coach you work your way up the ladder until you have earned the right and earned the experience to be a good head coach. I hadn't done any of that. As a result, I was not that successful. It was an embarrassment for me.

Pro Football Hall of Fame Induction
I was extremely honored and humbled by my induction. It's truly a unique honor when you're in something like that.

Favorite Moment In the NFL
I think my favorite moment that I had in the NFL was in the Ice Bowl and what that game meant to us. We had prepared so diligently for it and then to play under those conditions and along with those fellows. I am not exaggerating the ground was as hard as this desk that I'm sitting here tapping on right now. I don't know how we were able to do what we did or what Dallas did as well. It was very, very, very difficult to play that day.

It's a great challenge in a situation like that. I think that you call on your strengths and you have to have the right attitude. I personally feel that next to God, attitude is the strongest word in our vocabulary. I think in a situation like that, your attitude in a game where the ground is just almost frozen, and it is so cold it's unbelievable, that your attitude is going to be a very, very strong asset.

Green Bay Packer Bart Starr talks with Head Coach Vince Lombardi
Photograph copyright Associated Press

Chapter 20

Willie Davis

> College:
> Grambling State
>
> Career History:
> Cleveland Browns (1958-1959)
> Green Bay Packers (1960-1969)
>
> 1981 Inductee Pro Football Hall of Fame

College Choice
Actually, I went to Grambling State because of the coach more than anything. Coach Eddie Robinson, who as you know before he passed away, turned out to be the winningest coach ever. You'd only need to spend a couple of minutes with him to know why. He was the most dynamic man. He could make you feel like you were his only child for a moment, and the next moment he could make you realize that kickin' your butt was the best thing for you.

I was playing football in the South. Very, very few of the southern schools in the SEC and other places, were integrated. I never played against a team that had white players on it until I went to Cleveland.

Grambling
At Grambling Coach Eddie Robinson insisted that you not suffer in any situation for not getting the right information, the right style, or the right everything. He made it a point to make sure that every Grambling player was up-to-date. When I went to Cleveland, I didn't feel like I missed anything that any white player possibly would have done because I had covered it at Grambling.

Buck Buchanan & Willie Brown are in the Pro Football Hall of Fame from Grambling and there are a couple others that skip me right now. Coach Robinson at one time, had 13 players in the pros at the time. He truly was a coach probably ahead of his time.

First Training Camp With Cleveland Browns

Frankly, I didn't know what to expect. I was a little bit fearful of some of the challenges, but once I got there, I got acclimated. It's football any way you look at it. I remember Coach Eddie Robinson telling me when I was up at camp (he used to call me Big Dave), "Big Dave, how is it going?" I said, "Coach, it's going okay, but I feel like I spend half the time explaining where Grambling is." He said, "What?" I said, "I feel like I spend half the time with the players and the other half with other people explaining where Grambling is." There was a pause, and he said, "Well, let's give 'em a couple weeks. They'll know. They'll know."
I never forgot that because he was right. Within a month or so, everybody could appreciate Grambling.

Comparing Eddie Robinson & Paul Brown

Coach Paul Brown felt, we can show you, we can teach you, but we can't do it for you. He believed there was a certain amount you had to bring to the game, to practice, and everything else. I would say Coach Robinson had a similar opinion, but he would hand-feed you a little bit along the way. Coach Brown would say, "Hey, get out there and do it." And, he expected you to do that.

Otto Graham & Bart Starr

Otto Graham obviously had to have coaching along the way, but I think his mindset just led him to kind of always be reaching for that next level. He was always reaching for that next opportunity to do it better.

Many times I've said that if there was a player that in my mind reminded me of Otto Graham, it was Bart Starr. They had very similar habits and behavior. There was no one that wanted victory any more than Bart.

Trade to Green Bay Packers

My trade to the Green Bay Packers turned out probably to be a mistake for Cleveland to the extent that I went on and had the career that I had, but I never held it against Paul Brown. I just went out and tried to kick their butts and make sure that he remembered.

In fact, my Browns teammates used to tease me in training camp telling me if I didn't like it in Cleveland, they could always send me to the Siberia of football in Green Bay. Believe it or not, when I went to Green Bay, I could sense what players in Cleveland and other places would think. It was just not a team that was focused or was prepared each Sunday to go out and win. That's where Vince Lombardi came in. He changed all of that. With him, you went out every Sunday, or whatever day the game was, prepared to win.

Vince Lombardi
I have said this before, and I'll say it as long as I live that there's no question in my mind Vince Lombardi created more diversity in the National Football League than any coach ever. He brought black players in not thinking whether they were black or white. He was thinking can you play football and make us a better football team, then we want you on our team. I think to the very end he felt that he had accomplished something.

Position Change from Offensive Line to Defensive Line
There's no question that I was better suited playing defense because of my intensity and my speed. There were a lot of things that Coach Paul Brown just didn't recognize that Coach Vince Lombardi immediately saw and put in place.

Vince Lombardi Only Losing One Playoff Game As A Head Coach
He would probably say, "We didn't lose that game; time didn't permit us to win." He was right about the 1960 Championship. No question in my mind. That game ended with us down on about the 15-yard line. Give us another couple minutes and we would have scored. We probably would have won the football game. I always adhere to his thought that in some instances we didn't lose that game; time didn't permit us to win. They stopped Jim Taylor and Chuck Bednarik sat on him until the time ran out.

Sacks
It's probably unfortunate they didn't keep track of sacks. There's no question in my mind I would have been someplace north of 150-160.

Deacon Jones
Deacon Jones was a great rusher, but I can tell you that he had great support with Merlin Olsen, Rosey Grier, and Lamar Lundy. Many times a quarterback didn't have a place to go. Deacon, with his great speed and quickness, could get there. I know this: The times we played the Rams I remember one game they beat us. There is no question in my mind over the series that we played when I was there, I had more sacks than Deacon.

Five Championships
The five championships that I was a part of each had a special place. That first championship we won in Green Bay when we beat the New York Giants, was the sweetest because it was Vince Lombardi succeeding. It was the Packers succeeding. It was all the things that we probably wanted to accomplish in Green Bay at the time. It was a great feeling.

That championship clearly was a great moment in Vince Lombardi's life. Even in a private conversation he told me how much it meant for him to succeed. There's no question that as we went on and won other championships ... the first two Super Bowls were important to us ... but I'd have to go back and say that the victory against the Giants in the NFL Championship was probably as big as any.

Green Bay Packers Running Game
Our running game at the time was probably equal to our passing game. We threw when the situation required us to throw, but I think what we were all about was if we needed to move the ball we could run it. Jim Taylor and Paul Hornung probably were two of the best players of their time back then. They just wouldn't be denied.

Cleveland Browns Running Backs
When I left Cleveland, I talked about what a combination Jim Brown and Bobby Mitchell should have been. I still think about what would have happened, if Ernie Davis had lived, with Jim Brown. You probably

would have the record books today full of information covering the two of those guys.

Jim Brown
When people ask me could Jim Brown have played today, and it's almost like I have to look at them and say, Are you serious? Jim Brown as far as I'm concerned could have played in any era of football, including now, and anytime before.

Super Bowl I
It was kind of a strange game. In some ways we went into the game very conservative and very concerned that we did nothing to encourage Kansas City, and that was totally due to Coach Vince Lombardi. He sat us down one day and he said, Don't forget that when you look at their team roster, they have some of the same All-Americans and everybody else that you played against. I would say by game time he had us very concerned. We went out and to this day I will remember at halftime when we all had a moment to refresh, he got us together. He said, I just want to say a couple things. He said, "You went out and played 30 minutes of football, and you adjusted to the Chiefs. Now I want you to go and play 30 minutes of Green Bay Packer football and let's see can the Chiefs adjust to you." It was almost like he couldn't have been more profound. He said it, you had a sense that he felt it, and all at once we were a different team in the second half.

Favorite Play
I had that one tackle on Johnny Unitas when we beat them over in Baltimore the year that we won that second championship I believe it was. I hit Johnny Unitas and he fumbled. They called it the million dollar fumble. I always laughed. I said, Well, that's interesting. It was a million dollar fumble that was done by probably a $10,000 guy.

Baltimore Colt Johnny Unitas, watches Green Bay Packer Willie Davis, New York Giant Sam Huff, and New York Giant Frank Gifford jump off a tank during their visit to U.S. Installations in Saigon, South Viet Nam on Feb. 15, 1966. Photograph copyright Associated Press

Chapter 21

Tommy McDonald

> College:
> Oklahoma
>
> Career History:
> Philadelphia Eagles (1957-1963)
> Dallas Cowboys (1964)
> Los Angeles Rams (1965-1966)
> Atlanta Falcons (1967)
> Cleveland Browns (1968)
>
> 1998 Inductee Pro Football Hall of Fame

Favorite Quarterback
Norm Van Brocklin, Sonny Jurgensen, Roman Gabriel. Gosh, I was blessed. Absolutely blessed. I was in the right spot at the right time thanks to the good Lord. You know, God is my quarterback.

I had two great quarterbacks, Sonny Jurgensen and Norm Van Brocklin. It was great being there with them. We won the 1960 Championship against Green Bay and Vince Lombardi, Bart Starr and all of those guys.

Recipe for Success
God gave me good speed and good hands. Sports Illustrated put me on their cover in 1962 for having football's best hands! When that happened, I thought I better prove that I have the best hands. I used to squeeze clay to make my fingers strong. It really strengthened them. I was really lucky that made my fingers and hands strong.

My speed helped me too. I won the 100-yard DASH and the 220-yard DASH when I was in high school. I got a scholarship to the University of Oklahoma. I got about five scholarships offered to me from SMU, TCU, Texas, Oklahoma, and Colorado. I looked at SMU and Texas Christian, but I decided on Oklahoma because Bud Wilkinson said something that really hit home with me.

He said, "Now Tommy, if you're just coming here for football, I don't want you to come. I want you to come here to get an education because the education is going to last for the rest of your life. Football is only going to last for four years." I got to thinking, other coaches were thinking about the four years I was in school, but they weren't thinking about what happens to me afterward. That helped make my decision. What a beautiful decision. I went to Oklahoma and we never lost a game!

Bud Wilkinson
I won 10 games my sophomore year, 10 games my junior year, and 10 games my senior year. I made All-American at the halfback position. We played Notre Dame and beat them 40 to nothing. Paul Hornung was on that team.

Pro Football Hall of Fame Induction
I can't get over even getting into the Hall of Fame because I'm only 5'9". Nowadays, if you're only 5'9", they don't even want to give you a scholarship to college. You're told you're too little or you're too small. You have be 6'2" or 6'1" or something like that. But, low and behold, I was able to do that with Oklahoma.

The Eagles drafted me. During my rookie year with the Eagles, in 1957, our receiver broke his arm. They put me out there to see how I could do and I scored two touchdowns. They said, "Tommy, you're halfback days are over. You're going to be a receiver from now on."

That was really great. Low and behold, God just let me be in the right place on the right team. I'm very big on God because he's my quarterback every day. Every day is game day in life. You're either on God's team or the devil's team.

Chuck Bednarik
I'll tell you one thing, I wouldn't want to be hit by number 60, old Chuck Bednarik. He's just something else.

Mike Ditka
Mike Ditka, I love that guy. I would love to be on his team and have him coach me. Jiminy Christmas, what a desire that guy has. I'm so glad that he got in to the Hall of Fame too. In fact, he even beat me in the Hall of Fame. He got there in 1988; he beat me by 10 years, 1998.

Being Last Non Kicker to Not Wear a Facemask
I didn't wear a facemask, because I didn't want that bar to be in front of my face and in my eyes. I wanted to be able to see very clearly when that ball was coming into my hands and everything like that. I played for the Eagles for seven years before I got traded to the Dallas Cowboys, and that wasn't really good. They didn't really throw the ball a lot even though they had Don Meredith. I told Tom Landry after the season was over, "Coach, I'm out of here because you run the ball all the time. I'm a receiver; I want to be involved in the game a little bit. I would like to have one or two catches a game!"

Baltimore Colt Bobby Boyd defends Los Angeles Ram Tommy McDonald. Photograph copyright Associated Press

Chapter 22

Sonny Jurgensen

> College:
> Duke
>
> Career History:
> Philadelphia Eagles (1957–1963)
> Washington Redskins (1964–1974)
> 1983 Inductee Pro Football Hall of Fame

College
When I was at Duke we went up and played Ohio State and beat them. We beat Nebraska in the Orange Bowl. It was a good football program at the time. We didn't throw the ball. I only threw it 53 times my senior year in college.

The only people that were throwing the ball in that area were the guys in Georgia. They probably threw the ball more than anything else. I really thought about going to school there. It would have probably facilitated my professional career, because you know in that era you played both ways. I played safety. I was leading the nation in interceptions at one time, playing safety, but it was a different style of football then.

Early Years with Philadelphia Eagles
I started four or five games my rookie year and was 1-3. We beat Cleveland, Pittsburgh, and Washington Redskins in my three wins. Norm Van Brocklin wasn't there in 1957 when I went to Philadelphia. He came in 1958 as our quarterback.

He was there '58, '59 and '60. We weren't very good in '58. We only won two games. We won seven in '59, and we won the championship in '60. After he retired, he became a coach. Then, before we got on the field in 1961, Buck Shaw retired. Nick Skorich took over as Head Coach in '61, and we won ten games that year. We had a big year offensively.

NFL Draft
I learned a great deal. We didn't have a flanker and we didn't have a wide receiver when I was at Duke. It was a different style of football.

The Eagles offensive coordinator was the man who came to Duke to work with me because we hadn't thrown the ball a lot. He put me through a lot of drills that they do with quarterbacks. They still do them today, throwing different types of passes. That's why I was drafted in the fourth round. I was fortunate to get with the Eagles. They drafted, Jimmy Harris an All-American quarterback from Oklahoma at that time. They were looking for quarterbacks. They needed to get some people in that position and let them grow. I had the opportunity to be mentored by Van Brocklin, who was a legend. I learned a great deal from him about touch, looking people off, and just learning to play the position.

My colleague's coach actually recommended me to the Eagles. He said, "Boy, he's going to make a very good safety in the league." I said, "What? If you put me at safety I'm not going to last a week up there."

Chuck Bednarik
Chuck Bednarik was on my team. He was a great football player and a great leader, on the Eagles football team. He was the face of the Eagles until Van Brocklin came, and then you had two faces of the Eagles. It was great to be around people like that. The Eagles had an outstanding defense and legends of the game on it. He was quite a football player.

He was a perfectionist and an instinctive football player. So many times in playing, the defense was designed to do one thing and he would just do it. Bednarik's instincts would take him to the football and he would be going the wrong way, but he would make interceptions and go back the other way. He was a great instinctive player and obviously a very physical, dominating player in that era.

Quarterbacking
You use psychology, and all quarterbacks did, in the huddle. You know who wants the ball in a crucial situation whether it's a running back or a

receiver. You could be a running back who just got a stinger on the play before that, and he'd want a break for a play. You know, just block or something instead of giving him the ball; that he just hurt a shoulder or something.

The receiver is the same way. Can you beat this guy? We need to move the chains. Can you run this pass pattern? He'd say, "Yeah, I'll get him." You ask a lineman the same thing. We need a first down. Can you get this guy? Can you block him? And the running back ... you know, that's where the game was on the field. I mean, we were drawing plays in the dirt! Yeah it was a great. I'm glad I played in that particular era.

I had great receivers in Philadelphia too. Tommy McDonald, Pete Retzlaff, and Bobby Walston. Charley Taylor came in as a running back and he was great. I think Charley Taylor would have been in the Hall of Fame even if he had to play defensive, like if he had played cornerback. He was a great athlete. He started out as a halfback, but he was an undisciplined runner because he was running by the lineman instead of giving them an opportunity to block. They made him a receiver and he was a great receiver. The job of the quarterback, to this day, is to get the ball in your skilled player's hands and give them the opportunity to make plays. The quarterback can't do anything with a ball in his hand except get it to a skilled player; whether it's a running back or receiver.

I broadcasted games for the Washington Redskins after I retired. I've been in the radio booth since 1981. I did games when I retired in '74, working with CBS Sports. I still sit and look at defenses. You're reading defenses before the snap of the ball like you did as a quarterback. I think it helped me playing defense.

Bobby Mitchell
Bobby complimented Jim Brown. He was a great football player. He was so fast. You just got the ball in his hand as quickly as you could and let him do the rest. He was capable of going the distance at anytime. Cleveland also had a tight end who was an undersized tight end, even for that era, but he was an exceptional one with Jerry Smith.

Tommy McDonald

Tommy McDonald was about 5'10. He was a great receiver. If he could touch the ball he was going to catch it. He didn't drop many passes. He was a halfback coming out of Oklahoma who they made a receiver. He was fun. We came in together. He was drafted in the third round and I was drafted in the fourth round by the Eagles. We were very close friends, and still are to this day. I still see him. We had a lot of fun playing.

Favorite Receiver

The guy who was open, the guy who could get open, and the guy you knew you could depend on in a crunch. It was the guy that would make the catch when you needed it the most and was going to give you a 100%. Charley Taylor was probably the best athlete overall. He had strength, size, and speed. He was a devastating blocker, just a complete football player.

Toughest Defensive Player

The toughest defensive players were the ones who put your lights out. I don't think so much of individuals. I think of teams, like the Bears. The Bears were a great football team in that era. You also had the Giants. The Giants were a very sound football team. You know, when you consider the fact that they had Tom Landry coaching defense and Vince Lombardi coaching offense, they were difficult to play. Obviously the Browns played great team defense. The Giants were just getting into the flex defense that Dallas made very famous later on. The flex defense had four defensive linemen, two on the line and two were back. It was really a gap defense, everybody was responsible for a gap and they played it. The Giants had great players in Andy Robustelli, Jim Katcavage, Rosey Grier, Dick Modzelewski, and Sam Huff. I mean, the people that they had were great football players. You know, when you're playing against people like that, it was very difficult. Then with The Bears having Doug Atkins and Larry Morris and the people that they had there, it was difficult to play them and you had to battle them.

99 Yard Touchdown Pass

I think that touchdown pass was against Dick Butkus. I remember him chasing Jerry Allen. It wasn't a very long pass. In fact, I threw it about 30 yards but, they were in single coverage and Butkus ended up on the back coming out of the backfield. I just remember Dick chasing Jerry Allen. He wasn't going to catch him down the sidelines and I was thinking to myself at the time, 'I hope he doesn't spike the ball. If he does, Butkus is libel to kill him. He'll beat him for that touchdown.' And I said, "Please don't spike it. You don't want to get killed down there."

Butkus was a great football player. The intensity that he had on every single play. You didn't play anybody better than Butkus.

Dick Butkus, Chuck Bednarik, Sam Huff
People like Dick Butkus, Chuck Bednarik, Sam Huff, yes, they all need to get to anger management class.

What a classic matchup that was when the Giants faced the Browns. Jim Brown & Sam Huff both won when they played. They both knew who they were playing against and it was great to watch, especially when you weren't a part of it.

Jim Brown
Without question, Jim Brown was the greatest running back I've ever seen. I played with him in the '64 Pro Bowl, and he was head and shoulders above everybody else, in my opinion, all time. I can remember being at Duke University and my football coach told us to go up and watch Jim Brown's lacrosse game. We said, "What?" He said, "Go up and watch his lacrosse game. Duke's playing Syracuse."

And we went up to watch and saw Jimmy Brown play lacrosse and he just ran up and down the field knocking people over and they had to change the rules of lacrosse because of the way he played. They changed the rules because he was just devastating. He was an All-American Lacrosse player and he was the best, best I'd ever seen at that game.

Jim was so much stronger than all the running backs. In talking with him over the years about running the football, he was so smart knowing where all the lines of pursuit were coming. He could go around the end and be making cuts, anticipating where the pursuit angles were coming from the defenders. He didn't have to look, he knew where they would be and that's what made him exceptional. You can go back and watch.

Every time you saw him running the football you know it is something special.

Favorite Coach

Vince Lombardi was head and shoulders above the rest. I played for nine different head coaches in the 18 years that I played. Its very interesting when you hear today and you've heard of in the past of coaches with 700 page, 400 page playbooks. Vince Lombardi was the only coach I played for that simplified the game of football. We had few plays and it wasn't how many plays you could run, it was how well you ran each play. So, it's a matter of execution. If you execute, you don't need a lot of plays. It's making those plays work against any defense and that was Lombardi's philosophy. He didn't have a lot of plays, but what you did, you did right. He simplified the game, the keys, the passing game, and reading double coverage and zones and what have you. It made the game fun. In 1969 I had more fun and worked harder under him than any year in professional football.

I don't care where he was coaching he would have been and was a leader. He knew how to motivate. He'd have been successful at anything he did and he proved that.

He also coached high school basketball. He knew nothing about basketball. We had books and I think they won. He was just a leader and knew how to coach and was a great communicator.

I talked with Paul Horning, Bart Starr, Boyd Dowler, Max McGee, and other players that had played for Lombardi before he came to Washington and they said, "You will love him. You will love him because of the intense preparation you go through, you're never surprised on the field." It was great preparation. It was really fun and I knew we were very fortunate to have him for any length of time. We unfortunately only had him for a year.

Photograph copyright Associated Press

Chapter 23

Sam Huff

> College:
> West Virginia
>
> Career History:
> New York Giants (1956–1963)
> Washington Redskins (1964–1969)
>
> 1982 Inductee Pro Football Hall of Fame

Early Life
I went to college at West Virginia. I went to grade school outside of Fairmont, West Virginia. Then I went in West Virginia to Morgantown for high school.

My dad, my brothers, everybody went to work at Consolidated Coal Company. Consolidated Coal Company owned the house, and they owned the coal under the ground. Consolidated Coal Company owned everything. I did go down in the coal mines with my dad, and they had a big machine underground called the Sam Huff Special, named after me.

One day in the mine I said, "Dad, we got to get out of here. This is like a time bomb." He said, "Oh, I knew you would say that because you want to go to New York, and Washington and West Virginia … all of that. This is what I do." I said, "Dad, let's get the hell out of here." And we did. We got on this big elevator and we got out. That mine exploded and killed 93 miners. Ninety-three. Unbelievable. I knew every one of them. But that's the life you live.

Every linebacker would tell you, if you have the ball, we're going to take you down, that kind of talk. Joe Schmidt had it, Bill George had it; all the great ones had it. When they got Chris Hanburger he was the outside linebacker and I was the middle linebacker. Nobody broke through the line, because when they got to the line we got them. Both of us hit them. That's what people want to see. They want to see a contact sport called football and that was the sport we played back then. I loved it then, and I love it now. I broadcast now and it's great. I get paid for broadcasting. I mean, how do you beat that?

Switching To Defense Upon Joining Cowboys
Tom Landry switched me to defense. Tom Landry was a coach in New York for the Giants. After I played in the College All-Star game in Chicago, I went to New York to meet Tom Landry and the Giants staff.

We had Jim Lee Howell as Head Coach who was from Arkansas and loved to yell and scream like a lot of coaches do because they don't know what the hell your name is. Jim Lee Howell used to say, "Hey, you! Hey, you!" Lombardi just looked at me and he said, "What the hell is going on with you?" I said, "That guy is yelling at me." This kind of stuff goes in to the game that America loves.

Well, Landry took a little gamble on me because I came from the all-star game and I could run. I basically hit people even in practice. I knocked Jim Brown out. I knocked Jim Taylor out. Practice to me was just like a game. You came in my territory, I was going to deck you, and I did. That's what got me to where I am today, attitude, toughness, and a great coach by the name of Tom Landry. My other great coach was Vince Lombardi. Now, let me tell you something. It doesn't get any better than that.

Baltimore Colts
John Unitas called everything for Baltimore. Those big tackles, they didn't know what' was going on. They just knew to grab the defensive end and hold him.

1958 NFL Championship
Football is football. There's only one ball. Follow the ball. You have to have guys who take leadership in the locker room and on the football field. There are very few great coaches like Tom Landry and Vince Lombardi.

The Colts were a great team. That was a great match up between the two of us. It was a great game. Everybody got his money's worth at Yankee Stadium. There were Giant fans and there were Colt fans. That was a great contest.

I thought every game I played was the greatest game ever played. You go out there and you get hit. You get knocked down and you look up and here's a little guy about 135 pounds or something that blocked you. You just get up and you say, "Do that again and you ain't going to go home. Okay? I'll see to it." You put him on a train and send him to some place in New York.

Time Magazine Cover
I was the best player they could find for the cover of Time Magazine. I was the first and only one. People came to me and said, "We have a problem!" I said, "What's the problem?" They said, "Well, you're supposed to be on the cover of Time Magazine." I said, "Yeah. When do I have to do it?"

They were going to do it when they got rid of that monkey on the satellite. I said, "You mean to tell me I'm a football player and I tackle people and I got to answer to a monkey?" Honest to God. The monkey died and I'm on the cover of Time.

The guy from Time came to my locker at Yankee Stadium. I'm telling you stuff that nobody has asked before. He came to my locker. He said, "Sam, we got a problem." I said, "What are you talking about you got a problem?" He said, "Well, you're supposed to come out on Time Magazine." I said "Yeah, what's wrong with that?" He said "Well, there's a monkey that on the satellite and if that monkey dies, you are okay, but if that monkey lives, he's going on the cover." I said, "You mean to tell me I play football here in New York and I got to answer to a damn monkey?" Honestly, I'll tell you. The guy said, "Yeah, well." The monkey, he got lost and I was printed on the cover of Time Magazine. That's New York for you. It really is. It's the greatest city, to me, it's the greatest city in the world.

Jim Brown
Jim Brown was big and strong. I could take him down, and I did. I took down Jim Taylor too. They were great guys and great runners. We were blessed to have teams like the Giants and the Baltimore Colts and everybody else. Football is America's game.

Trade From New York Giants To Washington Redskins
It was the dumbest thing that ever happened to me. I was set with my family in New York, out by LaGuardia Airport and I gave them everything I had. I was on television with Howard Cosell. They made the mistake. We had a great team with great players and great coaches, playing in Yankee Stadium. We were champions. We played the best against the best all the time. That was the saddest thing, I think, other than death of my family, that's ever happened. To be traded. You're like a piece of equipment then. The Giants made a mistake when they started getting rid of people. They got rid of both Tom Landry and Vince Lombardi. Landry was defense, and Lombardi was offense. They were great. Why would they let them get away? That's where the Giants made their biggest mistake ever, in my opinion.

Howard Cosell
Howard Cosell was a yeller. He was like a fan. He loved television because it made him look good and he could yell and scream. He kept us on Monday Night Football with his yelling and screaming.

Vince Lombardi
Well, the best against the best. We played against the Green Bay Packers where Vince Lombardi was, when I was with the Giants. Lombardi was the best. He was like all of the great coaches. When he yelled, you moved. You got out of the way. He was a yeller and a screamer. The Giants had Tom Landry and Vince Lombardi as coaches and didn't hire either one of them. That was awful.

Chuck Bednarik Hit on Frank Gifford
That was the greatest hit I've ever seen. I mean Frank Gifford caused that himself. You're trained defensively to take a pass drop and Chuck Bednarik did. You're trained not to go underneath the linebacker. You're trained to go behind them because there's a seam in-between the linebacker that the quarterback would throw the ball to you. Well, Frank

came underneath two linebackers for the Philadelphia Eagles at Yankee Stadium and was running toward the pitcher's mound, because we shared that stadium. Bednarik hit him. It was the biggest hit I've ever seen. He clotheslined him. He flipped him in the air. Gifford came down, hit his head on the ground and fumbled the ball. The Eagles recovered it with two minutes to go in the game. I thought Gifford was dead. They carried him off the field on a stretcher and took him to the Yankee Stadium locker room.

I thought Chuck Bednarik killed Gifford. I walked over and Gifford was shaking. It was near the cut out on the field, I guess. I looked down at him and he was shaking. I told the umpire, "You got to be careful. I think he's going to die." That was the biggest hit I think I've ever seen on a football field

The Eagles recovered the ball and just ran out the clock. We went in the locker room and we were getting undressed. Andy Robustelli was on one side of me and they brought a body out of the trainer's room, covered up on a gurney with a sheet over it. I said, "There goes Gifford, he's dead. He's dead. Bednarik killed him!"

It wasn't Frank; it was a policeman who was working the game. He was so excited he had a heart attack and died. This all took place at Yankee Stadium. I thought it was Frank. It wasn't Frank, but unfortunately somebody died. Frank was already at the hospital. He was hit so hard he was knocked out. Frank missed the entire next season.

Frank was a heck of a ballplayer, but he made a mistake going underneath Bednarik. I would've done the same thing. Bill George would've done the same thing. Dick Butkus would've done the same thing. Butkus would've acted like Bednarik did, slamming his fists and all that kind of stuff. It was terrible, but it was football and you have to say, "That's the way I would've hit the guy too."

Frank is still alive. Frank is still Frank. I'm glad he's alive. He's a good person. He's a great person and he was a great player. We had some great players there, and Frank Gifford was one of them.

Chuck is a good guy but he liked to let everybody know how tough he was. Goes around hitting people. Hey, it's okay to hit somebody. Just make sure they have their uniform on. But, I'm not sure he knew that.

Pro Football Hall of Fame Induction
I made it. That's all you have to say. That's all you can say. When a coach tells you something, you do it or he'll get rid of you. That's the way you feel. It's a great event in Canton, Ohio. When you see people like Bobby Layne and Chuck Bednarik there; you see guys from every team that were on those football fields. Then here you are in Canton, Ohio and you're in a parade. It's something special.

Toughest Ball Player Went Up Against
There were two. Jim Brown and Jim Taylor. They were great. You're standing up. They're down in a three-point stance and you know that quarterback's going to hand that ball off because he doesn't want to get hit. Hand it off to Jim Brown and boy, you got to take him down quick or he's going down for a touchdown. Jim Taylor, from Green Bay, would hit you up to try to run over you. I took them both on.

Yankee Stadium & Mickey Mantle
I got a chance to play for the Giants in Yankee Stadium. I shared a locker with Mickey Mantle. It doesn't get any better than that. You could ride the train from downtown New York, where we all lived, to Yankee Stadium for a quarter. Hell, that was a lot of money then. You make do with what you got.

Favorite Player Growing Up
Frank Gatski was my favorite player. He played for the Cleveland Browns. Gatski was ahead of me in West Virginia. We played against each other. That's the kind of games that America has. You go out there and you play and you beat each other up, but you're still friends.

Most Memorable Play In Career
The game when I hit Jim Taylor in New York has to be my most memorable play. I hit him so hard I damaged his helmet and mine. Mine came down and split. The umpire said, "Sam, for Christ's sake, you destroyed your helmet!" And I said, "Well, for Christ's sake, get me another one."

The trainer saw what was happening. He got a new helmet and brought it out to me. He took the old one and threw it away. I had a new helmet. The helmet is like a military helmet, somewhat, I guess. Your helmet fits tight and it's got a strap underneath so you don't lose it. That helmet becomes a weapon in some people's mind. It's a weapon, because he's going to hit me with his helmet and I'm going to hit him with mine. That's the way the game was played.

Most of the guys on defense were pickups at one time or another. Frank Gifford came from California and he liked to be in Hollywood. Football is football. You put us on the field and people are going to get hit, people are going to get hurt. I hit Jim Brown and probably knocked him out. I hit Jim Taylor and probably knocked him out. I hit them so hard they had to get new helmets, too. So, there were three new helmets. I had a new helmet, Jim Brown had a new helmet, and Jim Taylor had a new helmet.

Success is success. I could hit people, I could tackle people, and I could cover people. A great linebacker, like Joe Smith, was one. He was the big guy in Philadelphia. We basically have our group. We played hard and we hit hard. That's what people pay to see. If they go to a prizefight, they want to see somebody box and hurt somebody. If you're in New York at Yankee Stadium, we're going to hit you down on the field. That's the way the game is played and it's okay. It's a great game. It's America's game.
I did my job. I dented a few helmets of my own hitting Jimmy Taylor and Jimmy Brown. It's like a car collision. You have a wreck but both sides are going to get hurt.

Tommy McDonald
Tommy never came over the middle. He ran the up pattern. It was a corner pattern but he didn't come over the middle. He was a good player.

Football in the 1950s
The Bears have always had good linebackers. Somehow they like that bad weather in Chicago. Those were such great days in the '50s with the Chicago Bears and the New York Giants. Sports were different then. Now, these guys make a play and what do they do? They bump their

rear-ends together and pump their shoulders together and show their muscles. If you did that with us, one of those linebackers would walk up there and punch you in the mouth.

Todays Players Celebrating After a Catch
I'll tell you what I'd do. I would take the 15-yard penalty and knock him into the stands. So would Chuck Bednarick, Bill George, Joe Schmidt, and all of us linebackers. We wouldn't put up with that crap. Excuse the language but that's true.

Well, that's because of coaching. Coaches control that. You would never do that with a Tom Landry or Vince Lombardi. These coaches allow that to go on. You just don't do that. You have to have control of these guys. There are about 100 of them. You throw a fine on them or cut their pay or get rid of them.

Jack Kent Cooke
Jack Kent Cooke drafted three quarterbacks in one year, Heath Shuler, Trent Green, and Gus Frerotte. Now, I live five minutes from Mr. Cook and you know I'm broadcasting and everything. He called me into his office and said, "I want to know, because you were a player, about these quarterbacks." He said, "We offered Heath Shuler a contract and I think it was about $500,000. The kid is just coming out of college. Sam, he's not going to report unless I give him a million. What do you think about that?"
I said, "Well, Mr. Cook, you drafted three quarterbacks and you've got to get your number one draft pick into practice and get him going. Why don't you talk to his agent." Now they all have agents, but we were not allowed to have one. They all have a lawyer and advisor and so forth now. I said, "Why don't you talk to his agent and tell him that he's the number one choice. If he takes you to the Super Bowl, you'll give him a million dollars."

You know what he said? "Get the hell out of my office! I ain't giving anybody a million dollars." He doesn't show up and they start out with Gus Frerotte. I'll never forget this. It was against the New York Giants at FedEx Field. He ran like a quarterback draw or something and goes into the end zone for a touchdown. He got so excited that he ran his head into the stadium.

I remember saying to Sonny Jurgensen, "I'm glad that was a quarterback instead of a linebacker because I'd never hear the end of it." He knocked himself out. I mean, things happened in Washington that were unexplainable sometimes.

The Violent World of Sam Huff on CBS
Oh well, I was wired for sound. They put a backpack on my shoulder pads and covered it up with sponge rubber. I had a microphone on the front of me. They recorded everything. That was CBS News. That was not CBS Sports. They recorded every hit that I made and every play that was called, and that was the big sounds. You know, it was award winning. That pack that they put on my back was a little over a pound. If you're playing, like I was playing, I was on all the special teams as well as the middle linebacker, it weighted me down a little bit but I was young and I was able to handle it. It was great. I didn't know how important it was. I just did what they asked me to do.

That was one of the deals that I made. You edit the film and cut out the bad language and they did that. It was really first class. CBS did it and they did such a great job. It won all kinds of awards. I was the first guy ever wired for sound. It was magnificent and it helped me get another raise of about 500 dollars.

I was in New York at the time and when you're in New York, all those big corporations there went to see the Giants play at Yankee Stadium. Now Yankee Stadium doesn't exist anymore. It's a different world. But, that was a great time in sports. As far as I'm concerned the '50s and the '60s made it what it is today and they are reaping the benefits of it.

New York Giant Sam Huff puts a crushing hit on Green Bay Packer
Jim Taylor
Photograph copyright Associated Press

Chapter 24

Don Maynard

> College:
> Texas Western
>
> Career History:
> New York Giants (1958)
> CFL Hamilton Tiger-Cats (CFL) (1959)
> New York Titans/Jets (1960-1972)
> St. Louis Cardinals (1973)
> Los Angeles Rams (1973)*
> WFL Houston Texans / Shreveport Steamer (1974)
>
> 1987 Inductee Pro Football Hall of Fame

College Choice
I went to Rice University first and I stayed down there a year. Then I transferred to Texas Western College in El Paso. I was home sick, lonesome, and 585 miles from home. I went home five times the first semester and rode a Greyhound bus 585 miles. Each time I went home, I went home to stay, but my brother got on my case and I went back. Eventually I stayed and transferred my hours to Texas Western College. I was a redshirt out there during spring training and then the next fall. Being on the redshirt team I did everything. I played quarterback and so forth. When I got eligible as a sophomore, I stepped into the starting lineup and was a starter for three years. Back then, you played both ways. Defense was my claim to fame, but I did pretty well on offense, too.

NFL Draft
The Giants drafted me and I belonged to them. I went to the Giants in '58 and we wound up going into the sudden death game with the Colts. I ran kickoffs back and I did punt returns. I was probably one of the most versatile players on the team besides the great Frank Gifford.

First Training Camp
My first training camp was in Salem, Oregon. The name of the college was Willamette University. In training camp, there's not too much going on.

Accommodations During Season
I lived in the same hotel as Frank Gifford and Charlie Connelly. There were about 18 Giants that lived at the Concourse Plaza Hotel. We went to workout every day. We had to be in our seats and ready to go at 12 o'clock. Then we had meetings and practice. After practice we got home about 5:30. Like I say, many families lived in the hotel.

The Concourse Plaza Hotel was one of the old established hotels. It was about two or three blocks up from Yankee Stadium and across from the Polo Grounds. They had apartments in the hotels. You could have a one room efficiency that had the kitchen on one wall and the couches made into beds. If you had kids, you might have a one bedroom. Maybe if somebody's got more, they might have a two bedroom. There were all kinds of suites, but they all had a full kitchen and bathroom facilities.

Everybody was pretty close. I think we only had three rookies on the ball club, so the veterans were real close. That was my first year in '58, that they put 35 players on the roster.

1958 New York Giants
The enjoyment is you played your position. You did what you were told to do on the field and that was it. We probably had the most players ever from one team to have made it into the Hall of Fame.

Vince Lombardi
Vince Lombardi was a great coach. He was probably as great as he was back then with the Giants as he was later with the Packers. A lot of his greatness carried over and that's why he became the head coach at Green Bay. The nice thing about him and Tom Landry was they expected you to know the system, and they wouldn't tolerate a mistake. There weren't any mistakes made. I think I made one, one time in a ballgame. I was supposed to fake up into the line a little bit. Charlie Connerly was

throwing a delayed flare or swing pass to the back, and I missed it. That was the only mistake I made in 16 years of pro football.

1958 NFL Championship Game
We were tied with Cleveland in the Eastern Division and played them in a playoff. We beat them and went to the championship game. Years later, I knew if we just showed up we were going to get the losers share and if we played a little harder, we could wind up with the winning share. The Baltimore Colts had a great team led by Johnny Unitas, Raymond Berry, and some other great players who wound up in the Hall of Fame. That game probably had more Hall of Fame guys in it than any game that will ever be played. When we went into overtime, it proved which team was the best team. That day Baltimore was the best.

Whatever Frank Gifford said and whatever the film showed regarding Frank Gifford and him missing the first down, the nice thing about film, a lot of times it answers the truth. Frank said the officials missed him getting the first down. He had carried the ball and that's the play that one of the Colts, Gino Marchetti, broke his leg on and there was a lot of confusion going back and forth with the officials in trying to get a trainer out to the injured player. I'm sure he's seen it a lot more times than I have, but whatever he said was probably true.

Being Cut by Giants Before 1959 Season
That was in 1959 during training camp. Vince Lombardi went to Green Bay and Tom Landry went to Dallas after the 1958 season and the Giants brought in a guy named Allie Sherman. He had been on the Giants scouting staff and he had been a coach. He's the guy that cut me. I never dropped any balls and never said anything to anybody. They kept somebody in the place of me. I could have probably run backwards faster than that guy could run forward. When a coach doesn't like you, then you've got a problem. The nice thing about Landry and Lombardi was that they always kept the best ballplayer. It wasn't the case with Allie Sherman. It tickled me years later when he became a head coach and he probably lost a bunch of games.

I played under nine head coaches and 42 assistants. I only complain about one, and that's Allie Sherman. As time went on, I found out that I knew a lot more about football, especially about the passing game, than he'd ever know.

I got released by the Giants and instead of going home, I made contact with the Hamilton people and decided to just run up there and play. I could play as a wide receiver and also go both ways. They had 12 Americans; most of the 12 Americans went both ways, except the quarterback position.

After I went up there, I learned that Lombardi had picked up my option in Green Bay. I had already played a couple of games before they finally tracked me down. I mentioned to Vince Lombard that I was getting to play up there. Under contract rules, I would have had to go back to Green Bay, but Lombardi was nice enough to say, "If you're doing okay, I won't contest the agreement between the Canadian League and the NFL." So I stayed there and went to the Grey Cup. We lost to Winnipeg in the Grey Cup. A coincidence, 20 some years later my son wound up coaching for Winnipeg. They won the Grey Cup and were also runner up. He has a ring a lot bigger than my Super Bowl ring.

New York Jets
In 1960, the American Football League was founded. When I played in Canada, I didn't sign a contract to go back until the next year. When the American Football League was founded, I wound up being the first New York Titan that was signed. The Titans later became the Jets. I stayed with the Jets for 15 years.

The Green Bay Packers had given me my freedom, a free release so to speak, and they wouldn't contest it. I wanted to play with the New York Titans because they hired Sammy Baugh as coach. I had played against him when he was a coach my three years in college and I played for him in the Blue-Grey game. I knew he was going to throw the ball a lot. His key receiver coach was Bones Taylor. Bones told me they were just going to have me play offense, wide receiver, and that's the way it turned out there.

I think we were the number one or two team in the league in yardage gained. I was right up there one or two from the top with the most receptions. We had a good passing attack.

Sammy Baugh

Sammy Baugh was the greatest guy. He's probably the greatest football player who ever played. People talk about Jim Brown being a great player. I came up with a point deal with players. Let's say offense is 10 points, defense is 10 points, and punting is 10 points. Sammy Baugh was All Pro offense, All-Pro defense, and his punting records probably still stand. He had 30 points compared to somebody else that might only have 10.

Jim Brown's a nice guy and a great runner, but on defense, I think he only played a little bit of defense in one game. He didn't run kickoffs or punts back, except maybe one game or two. Sammy Baugh was a great player, but he was also a great coach. He knew the offense, the defense and the passing game. It was great to be able to be indoctrinated into football under his ability. I played against him three years in college and I knew he was going to throw the ball. That's probably the main reason I came back to the states for the first year of the New York Titans and it was a lot of fun.

Joe Namath

Joe Namath played in the Bowl game against Texas. Naturally I watched TV and ball games. I could tell he was a great quarterback and then the Jets drafted him. He came to camp and I told him, "I'm going to make you a lot better quarterback and you're going to make me a great receiver. We're going to talk on every play in practice as we set up our passing offense."

Joe got to camp and we discussed a lot of things. I already knew he was a great ballplayer. I said, "We'll visit and we'll discuss the routes. I rounded my patterns off and that was a little bit different than some people were taught. It's like driving a pickup. When you drive a pickup, if you're going to turn 90 degrees to the right, you slow down. Me, I'm going to round mine, my pass pattern. Namath and I had one busted play in the 11 years we played together.

He called the plays in the huddle. I taught Joe something that I've never known a coach to teach. Joe calls a play. Let's say I'm going to run a 5-yard out. He knows I'm going to run a 5-yard out, but as he drops back in the huddle the defensive back comes up on me. As I call it, they used to call it bump and run. I call it the crowd. He's crowding me up on the line of scrimmage.

Instead of me running a 5-yard out, I'm just going to slide to the outside and I'm going to run a go pattern and he would just lay the ball up. I said, "Joe, don't read me. You already know what you told me to do. You read the defensive back. If he stays back 5-yards, I'm going to do a 5-yard out. If he comes up on the line of scrimmage, I slide to the outside and I'll run a go and we've got six points."

We went to the Super Bowl. Baltimore's defense doubled and tripled me the whole game. Namath wasn't going to throw the ball over to me, he just looked over and I'm out so wide, they've got to double and triple me so why even risk a throw over there? He threw about eight of the passes to Sauer, Mattress had three, Snell had maybe four or five, and Boozer had three or four.

Joe was just going to go to the guy who was open. Like I say, why risk throwing the ball to me when there were three guys guarding me? That worked out great. I always kid people and say, "I had the best seat in the house. I knew I wasn't going to get thrown to, but I had a job to do to entertain, the linebacker, a cornerback, and maybe a safety. It worked out real good."

Joe Namath's Prediction That Jets Would Win Super Bowl

We didn't even think about it. Matter of fact, all week long Pete Lammons said our defense was number one in the league and we had an offense that nobody was going to stop. We weren't worried about the Colts at all. We just did one thing. We didn't make any mistakes. As a result, that's the way it went and the game went a certain way. In the fourth quarter, I think it was 16-0, and Namath never even threw one pass in the fourth quarter. We just ran the ball down their throat. We had two of the greatest runners in the league, Matt Snell and Emerson Boozer. They did okay. As a matter of fact, I don't have some of the stats in front of me, but Matt gained over 100 yards. They never did slow him down.

His Speed
I don't know if anybody was faster than me. Many say they were a certain speed and they ran on a nice turf. I could run. I started out at about a 4.3 with full football gear on a grass field. We usually had our timing after a hard day's work out. Like I said, I never got caught from behind that's all that really matters.

Jersey Number 13
I chose 13 and even had it written in my contract with the Giants because I had worn it in college. The number 13 was a great part of my life. My dad was born on the 13th, my sister was born on the 13th, and I married a lady who was born on the 13th. I had 13 in college and I went to 13 schools growing up, five high schools. The Super Bowl victory was the 13th of the year. I just had all kinds of other 13's. I don't have my little chart in front of me to rattle off a whole bunch of deals, but I went to the Blue-Grey game and they never had a 13 in their history. I said, "I have to have 13 if I'm going to play in your game." They got me a jersey with a 13 on it.

I played for 13 years. "M" is the 13th letter of the alphabet. My mother and dad always called me Donald Maynard, which has 13 letters between my first and last names. I was number 139 going into the Hall of Fame. It's got a 13 in it and if you multiply 13 times 3, it will equal the 39, the end of that number.

Pro Football Hall of Fame Induction
I met some great guys playing football. All of the guys I was in the league with were deserving. As a matter of fact, I remember when we got to Canton, there was a big sign up that said exit number 13. When I saw the number 13 on that exit I said, "Well, I guess I'm supposed to be here." That worked out pretty good.

Philosophy

I never thought past the game that I was playing. A lot of times the only thing I'd look for on the schedule was when we might be going to Dallas to play them since it was in the state where I was raised. As a matter of fact, playing in the AFL championship, we played Oakland in New York. After the first half when we came in at halftime, I just said, "Men, if you want to go to the Super Bowl, you've got to win this game. The Super Bowl is in the future and it may not be there. We've got to go out there and play the second half like it was the only game we were playing." We did and we came back and beat Oakland. We all got to go to the Super Bowl.

If you want to go out there, it's just another ballgame. We're going to get paid the loser share just for showing up. If we go out there and play real well, we get the winners share. Somebody said they gave you a dime.

Then one guy said you get a check. I said, "I don't want a check. I want all my money in dimes. I want to see it. It worked out pretty good."

Favorite Moment

The big pass that made a lot of difference to me was in the playoff game against Oakland. In the third quarter, I said to Joe Namath I've got a wide one when you need it. It was late in the quarter. They got ahead. I ran a long go pattern and Joe told everybody in the huddle, "All right let's be careful. We're going to go for it. I need a little extra time, I just need for you to block them."

The wind was blowing about 50 miles an hour. I went down the right side, straight down the right side on a go pattern or post pattern and the ball was thrown at the post and I was behind the guy by about 3 or 4 yards. Then the wind caught the ball and if you're looking at a clock, I was going to catch it about 10 o'clock up there as you look at the clock as you run down the field. The wind caught the ball and it moved the ball over to the 11 and then 12 and then 1 o'clock or 2 o'clock right there. I caught it for 59 yards and went out of bounds at the 6 yard line.

My momentum and direction carried me out on the 6-yard line or I could have scored.

Then Joe called a couple of plays. He called a pass play to be on the right side, but then as the formation changed, the defense changed, instead of me being the number one option, now I'm number four in order of catching the ball. He went to the left looking to George Sauer and then Pete Lammons and then Bill Mathis and then to me. You could see him brace himself real strong. He threw the ball to me and I had done my delayed route to come open as the fourth receiver. He threw the ball and I caught it just about waist high and I just huddled it in and wound up and caught it for a touchdown. That put us back ahead of the Raiders and the defense held the Raiders down intercepting a ball I believe. We beat them for the AFL Championship to get to go to the Super Bowl.

Singing Career

That was a great time. As a matter of fact, later on Bake Turner recorded a song "Is Anybody Going to San Antone", and it was climbing the charts like mad. Our buddy Charlie Pride recorded it and he took it to number one. I think it was number one for about 20 weeks. Bake was a great entertainer. Getting on the Johnny Carson show and a couple other special event things that we went to, worked out really good. The other great thing is we got paid for it.

End of Career

I didn't call it a career. The last eight years I played, I didn't miss a pass. They brought in a couple of other guys. Weeb Ewbank brought in his son-in-law as an assistant coach and they just released me. Then I went to the Cardinals and after that, I went to the Rams. I told the Cardinals coach I wasn't going to be a messenger boy, sending plays in and out. I'm going to play regularly or you can cut me or trade me. The Cardinals released me.

I told their coaching staff what was kind of wrong with some of their ball players, the organization, and passing routes before I left. Then Don Coryell did pretty good there. After that he went to, I believe, the Chargers, but that was about it.

The politics got in there and so I didn't go back out to the Rams, which I should have.

Pro Football Hall of Fame Induction
I was real proud and glad. Joe Namath had gotten in a couple years before, I think. I went in '87. It's an honor to get in, but the main thing I felt good about was I was always in my mom and dad's hall of fame and my brother and sister's. Those were the main things with me and then naturally, my wife before I lost her.

New York Jet Don Maynard left with Joe Namath
Photograph copyright Associated Press

Chapter 25

Bobby Mitchell

> College:
> University of Illinois
>
> Career History:
> Cleveland Browns (1958-1961)
> Washington Redskins (1962-1968)
>
> 1983 Inductee Pro Football Hall of Fame

<u>College Choice</u>
It was the times. In the '50s I couldn't go to the University of Arkansas so I had to go east. Quite a few of us did that. You look at the Southwest Conference at that time or the Southeastern Conference at that time and African Americans weren't on any of those teams. The Big Ten had a long history going way back with African Americans. I didn't have much to do with my college choice. My mother, spoke to someone she knew in my hometown and he was an Illinois graduate. I didn't even know any of this, although I was around. He and the freshman coach at the university at the time had been roommates at Illinois. They had been following me all along. When everything opened up east and west in '54 with the Brown vs. Board of Education decision I went from five scholarships to something like 36. So, that's what happened. A lot of the schools opened up for blacks. They directed me to Illinois. To tell you the truth, I wanted to go to Grambling with Eddie Robinson.

All the black schools recruited me and none of the white schools recruited me. As I said, in '54, when the new school decision of Brown vs. Board of Education a lot of the schools opened up for blacks, that's when I got all of my scholarships at the last minute and had a lot of offers. My family had already decided I was going to Illinois. I didn't even know where it was. I said where is that? I had never been out of the south. I didn't know anything. So, that's how it happened. I ended up there not because I wanted that or that they had pursued me. It was really word of mouth and they gave me an opportunity so I took it. But, I was virtually controlled on that by my momma because I personally was going to Grambling.

Well, the one good thing I did that I often talk about, was go to the University of Illinois. I don't think that I could have made the Grambling football team. They had so many great football players because the guys couldn't go to white schools. They were just stacked up at those black schools. You couldn't get in to Florida, A&M, Jackson State, or Tennessee State. They had so many great athletes. I don't know what would have happened if I had gone to Grambling. Of course Eddie Robinson and I laughed about it for years. He had some great players, super, super players. So, I don't know what would have happened.

All of us coming out of Arkansas that year, the big time players, went east and my best rival and friend from Little Rock, Arkansas went to Michigan. He was an All-American at Michigan and he was everything up there. Another one of our guys from Little Rock went to Wisconsin. He probably was the first black quarterback out there, Sidney Williams. Michigan State got Smitty and different guys just went all over the country. They all did quite well. They all got great honors in their careers. I've always thought that I was the one that had the least chance of being a star because I didn't think that I was on the level of those guys but it worked out pretty good.

Grambling Pro Football Hall of Famers Willie Davis, Buck Buchanan, Willie Brown, & Charlie Joiner

Those are all good friends of mine. They all did real well. Willie Davis and I played together at Cleveland for a year and then he went to Green Bay. Later on, Willie Brown and I, if Al Davis could have pulled it off, would've been in Oakland together. We had some great guys come out of there. There were tons of other guys who did well in pro football. None of them are in the Hall of Fame, but several of them said they were good enough to get in the Hall. We had some great guys come out of Arkansas.

Draft

Well, you know the strange thing about it, I didn't know anything about pro football. I had never even watched a pro football game. All the time I was at Illinois I had never thought about pro football because I wasn't that good of a player at Illinois. Ray Nitschke wasn't either. All of us just came along at the last minute. I knew nothing about pro ball. I knew nothing about the Cleveland Browns. I was not contacted about pro football until the season was just about over my senior year. That's when a scout approached me and told me that Paul Brown of the Browns was interested in me. He wanted to know if I was interested.

I was sort of interested. I think that I had watched one game because J.C. Caroline went to the Bears and he was always playing defense and special teams. I wanted to watch him because I got to know him my freshman year at Illinois. That's the only reason I watched that one game. It wasn't on my mind. It was not even a part of my thoughts or anything like that. In fact, I didn't think that I could even play. I didn't think that I was good enough to go any further with my football career because I had become so enthralled with track. I was enjoying my track career at Illinois. I forget about football.

Let me say this, one of the things that has always disturbed me is that I didn't give it my all to the University of Illinois and the coaches because I never cared that much about football. I cared about track. I had a great sophomore year in football the last half of the season when I got a chance to play. When I played I had three, four, or five really great games my sophomore year. I got hurt my junior year. My senior year I was running well at track and didn't care. So, it was kind of a crazy, crazy, crazy career, college wise. So, I wish now that I had given my all for them because they could've used it. We didn't win very many games.

College All-Star Game

I thought that I might get a chance to go to the Senior Bowl because they selected Ray Nitschke and I think another receiver from Illinois. No blacks could play in the senior bowl that year so I couldn't go to it.

Later on, I was asked to go to the East-West game in San Francisco. Paul Brown had a friend who was coaching in the game invite me so that he could get a look at me. I had a very good game. I was shocked. When I got back to school, I found out that Paul Brown had also called Otto Graham who was the coach of the College All-Star team, to see if he could get me into the game. He wanted to look at me further. That's how I got invited to those two games.

The running back at Notre Dame had hurt his knee. Because he got hurt, Otto put me in his spot for Paul Brown and that's how I got into that game. I had never been outside as a receiver and they put me outside. I broke out and went on to have a tremendous game. That started my career. That's when the league was much smaller.

Cleveland Browns
I was in a fog after being drafted. I knew nothing about nothing. I was just being pushed along by people saying, "Now go here, and do this, and do that." Paul Brown sent me a contract and told me to read it, sign it, and get moving. After I had that game, the very next day, I had to report to training camp with the Browns.

It was the strangest feeling to walk into that dressing room at training camp. By then I had gathered some names, like Lou Groza and Jim Brown. I had to walk in that locker room and my eyes were running around. I was actually looking at these guys that I had been hearing about. I thought, what am I doing here? This is the Cleveland Browns and these are the greatest guys. It was a real shock. I had that great game but it just dawned on me that I could play with these guys.

I had to earn my way in training camp because they had a lot of good running backs when I got there. I was the rookie. They had a lot of veteran guys. Back then, there weren't very many teams. All of those teams had guys stacked up in positions waiting for an opportunity. A lot of them had already played for two, three, four or five years. So, you're up against a veteran player and trying to get a slot. I was just like a little kid. I didn't know what was going on. I was just running around. What settled me down was Paul Brown putting me in the same locker with Jim Brown. I didn't think that I had the right to be in that locker room with Jim Brown. But, the team accepted me. What saved me again was my speed. He didn't have anybody on the team that could run like me, speedwise. They had great players. I think that there was no doubt of my speed and that helped me.

Jim Brown
Well, for me, he was super because he kept me grounded and I just followed his lead. We were running mates and we were running buddies off the field. For four years we virtually lived together. So, we were very close.

Trade
Nobody was able to beat Green Bay. They had two big running backs, Jim Taylor and Paul Hornung. That always bothered Paul Brown because he had Jim Brown. He thought I was too small to go up in the middle, which wasn't true, but that's how he felt. He didn't run me in the middle that much. I had to get my yardage elsewhere. I think that had a lot to do with it.

Coming out of school that year was a young man who was big and built like Jim Brown and had some of Jim's speed. His name was Ernie Davis. I think that Paul Brown felt that he would go to the Redskins. They had the first pick that year and got Ernie, but Ernie didn't want to go there because of the situation of no blacks being there. It all worked out for Paul in that sense. He made the deal with the Redskins and said that they had to take a black and I guess they decided I would be a good one to have because I had beat them two or three times. So, the deal was laid that Ernie Davis would go to the Browns and I would go to the Redskins along with some other people. That's the way it went.

Ernie Davis got leukemia that summer and of course never got a chance to play. I really think that he would have been a great player.

I had been in the service when I was traded. Back then, the draft was in December so I was in service when everything went down. I really didn't know anything about the trade. It was told to me. I got out of the service just before training camp. That was the last year that the Redskins trained in California. George Preston Marshall always went out there to hang with the movie stars during the summer, so he would take the team out on the train and they'd train at Occidental College.

I went out there to hook up with the team. I remember, because I was a little late from the military. Bill McPeak was the head coach and I walked up a hill to the football practice field. When I got up the hill, nobody was there. This shocked me because with Paul Brown's team, you better be up there 30 minutes ahead of him. I couldn't believe there were no players there. It was probably five minutes before practice was going to start. That shocked me and then right away I thought that's why they didn't win but one game last year.

Bill and I were standing there talking waiting for the players and he said, "Bobby, you know I don't have a great offensive line. I've got a good quarterback in Norm Snead. What do you think about (I'm sure that he and the coaches had talked about this.) going outside as a receiver."

I had never been a receiver and knowing that he didn't have a good offensive line, I didn't want to get killed either. I said, "Yeah, I'll try it." That's basically how that happened. From day one I went outside. The craziest thing about it was we didn't even have a receiver coach. I was basically coaching myself. I did a pretty good job for me to make All-Pro.

Another fortunate thing was back then, we had six preseason games. I needed all six of those games to get used to Snead and for Snead to get used to me, because we were training ourselves. Fortunately, by the last preseason game we began to find each other. That was just before the season so we went on and had a really good year.

1st Black Player with Redskins
What I went through, I wouldn't want for anyone. I think that if I had gone to the Redskins fresh out of college, there was a chance that I would've never made it because I couldn't have mentally handled all the things away from the game. It was a pretty tough town at that time. There were so many places you couldn't go. So many things you couldn't do. Because I had already been in the league for four years, I was kind of a seasoned veteran, and I had been virtually raised by Jim Brown. So, I had a stronger mind and I withstood a lot of the things that were going on. I don't think that I would've been able to make it if I had come fresh from college.

I think Ernie Davis was smart for refusing to go. I don't know if he would've been able to handle all the other things away from football. I had had four years of experience that helped me. I was able to disregard things and think about my family. It was pretty nasty at times. The players were great, but everybody around us was not. It was a pretty tough time.

They got blacks coming into the stadium which none had before. George Preston Marshall got financially better and the team was better. The rah, rah, rah was better. Everything just went top-side. The only thing was that the black guys had a tough time.

George Preston Marshall
People wonder about him because of his reputation and what it was like, but there was not much contact with him other than when I first met him. We talked and finely agreed on a contract. After that, I really didn't see him that much. I would see him once a while since he was the owner. Players don't spend that much time around owners. Today they do a little more because everybody is a publicity hound, but back then you didn't see owners that much. The coaches didn't want them around anyway because they wanted to control their players and their team. So, I never really had that much interaction with George Preston Marshall. I was like everybody else. I was hearing about him and I'd see him and he would speak, but I didn't have much interaction with him.

Being Switched To Wide Receiver
Otto Graham always said I was his best runner because he knew me from the Browns. He didn't like not being able to use me in the backfield. When he would bring it up, I would refuse it. So, what he would do was wait until the game would start and then send in a play for me to go to the backfield. Well, every time he'd do that, I'd either break it for a touchdown or for a very long run. This was really playing right in to his hands, that he was right. I was his best running back. But, I had gotten used to being outside as a receiver and I liked it. I didn't want to go back in the backfield. The guy that I watched all the time, Lenny Moore, who went from running to receiver and then back to runner, popped his kneecap. I was thinking about that as soon as he went back to the backfield. I didn't want to get hurt back there and ruin my career. But he insisted on it and so I had to run in the backfields sometime and

play outside sometimes. We would try to harness Charlie Taylor's speed and quickness, but he was too fast for the linemen. He didn't know how to adjust to it. It was better for Charlie to go outside where he could go on and cut loose. Of course he went on and was one of the greatest receivers.

No one wanted to decide where I should be. I was returning punts and kicks. I was too versatile.

Pro Football Hall of Fame Induction
Reporters talked to me about why it took me so long to get into the Hall. It was that all of my votes were being split up. A certain number of reporters wanted me in as a runner, another group as a receiver, and others wanted me in as a special teamer. Finally, they agreed to combine it all. When they did that, I went right in to the Hall. My chances were getting hurt because I was too versatile.

When you're name comes up as a possibility you're excited. Then it took nine years to get in. That's what happened in my case. It's year after year of being disappointed, which as you know today, is happening to so many guys.

You're on that list each year and you never can get in. You get close but never in. Each year that you don't get in, there are great players coming up.

On Not Being Named A General Manager
When you're ahead of your time, you can't be bitter about something like that. I was never bitter about that. I knew all along that it wasn't going to happen even though I knew Mr. Cooke respected me very much. He called on me too many times to do things that he would normally ask other people in the hierarchy to do, so I knew that he respected me and he respected my brain power. He was no different than most of the owners in the league at that time. Who wanted to be the first to make that move? I never expected it to happen, though. It never really bothered me. It bothered other people. It bothered people in the organization. It was something that I didn't have to get because I had learned as an assistant general manager I had all the power that I needed.

Washington Redskin Bobby Mitchell makes leaping catch over St. Louis Cardinal Norman Beal

Photograph copyright Associated Press

Chapter 26

Len Dawson

> College:
> Purdue
>
> Career History:
> Pittsburgh Steelers (1957-1959)
> Cleveland Browns (1960-1961)
> Dallas Texans/Kansas City Chiefs (1962-1975)
>
> 1987 Inductee Pro Football Hall of Fame

<u>College Choice</u>
Woodie Hayes was recruiting me and he basically said, "You're an Ohio guy. You gotta come to Ohio State. I'll teach you the split pea." I said "What is that?" "Well, he said, you're in the center with three backs behind you. You take the ball and step into the line of scrimmage." That got my attention. In the line of scrimmage?

He said, "So the back will dive into the line of scrimmage. You either hand it off to him or you continue down the line of scrimmage. We'll option off of that defensive end." I said, "What do you mean option." He said, "Well, we're not going to block you. If he comes for you, you pitch it back to the trailing back. If he goes after the back, then you carry it."

I started thinking about my health being in the hands of some big defensive lineman. I don't think so. I went to Purdue and they showed me the highlight film of their passing game and every one was a completion. So, I said "This is where I want to go. Purdue University."

NFL Draft

I was drafted number one by the Steelers in '57. In '56, Detroit won the championship, and they beat Cleveland. They were going to have a luncheon before they went to training camp and Buddy Parker said, "Now listen I don't want anybody above the mezzanine floor because there are going to be some hospitality suites by corporations here. There will be drinking going on, so let's get this luncheon over with. Bank 'em, and we will get on and try to defend our championship."

Buddy got on the elevator and instead of stopping at the mezzanine it went all the way up to about the 15th floor. The elevator doors opened up to a suite there. He saw a couple of his players having a tottie. So when they asked him to speak he said, "Listen, I can't control these guys anymore. I quit."

They thought he was joking but he wasn't, and so he left. Then Art Rooney called and said, "Listen, Buddy, Walt Kiesling is a friend of mine. He is coach here, but he has some health problems. Would you consider coaching the Pittsburg Steelers?"

He said yes, and came over from Detroit to Pittsburgh. He had never played a rookie in his life, and particularly a quarterback. So, he made a trade for Earl Morrall, who was with San Francisco, and I was Earl's backup. The next year they made a trade for Bobby Layne in Detroit, and I was his backup for two years. I didn't get to play. Then I went up to Cleveland to watch Milt Plum as quarterback, but I mostly watched Jim Brown and Bobby Mitchell run.

Jim Brown

Jim Brown was phenomenal. I've never seen anything like Jim Brown. Jim Brown never stepped out of bounds and the defensive backs weren't that big in those days. He was about 230 or 235 with great speed. They'd want to wait until he was even with them and then they would jump on his back. Well, hell, when he's even he's leading.

Super Bowl IV

We had to go to New York for the playoffs in '70, to play the Jets who had won the Super Bowl the year before. Otis Taylor made the big play there. He came to the sidelines. I know this doesn't happen anymore because the quarterback has a telephone in his ear, or you know, whatever that is, getting instructions from somebody. Otis is drawing, I have a photograph of it, a play in the dirt of what he thought he could do against the Jets. We used to create formations and we would create a slot formation. When we did that we had both wide receivers on the same side. He said, "If you go on a quick count, I can get down the field because it's not a cornerback that's covering me there. It's the free safety and I can beat him."

So we had a goal line stand, Namath threw a ball into the end zone incomplete but they threw the flag and it was interference first and goal. Our defense was Willie Lanier, Buck Buchanan, Bobby Bell, and those guys. They settled for a field goal. As we're going on the field after we got the kick off, Otis says, "Are you going to call that play? I said "No, no I'm not. I'm not gonna call it right now." I waited until we were in the huddle so everybody could hear me. Using my sense of humor I said, "Well hell yes, I'm going to call it." He was absolutely right and the wind was swirling there. If you didn't get a good release on the ball the wind would take it and move it wherever it wanted to. I let it go and I thought dogonit, I've threw it too far. But he had different gears in him so he caught up to it, took it inside the 10, and the next play we scored a touchdown. That was the difference in winning and losing that game. The next week we went to Oakland to play them. They had beaten us twice during the regular season. We beat them and he came up with the big play in that game. Man, a marvelous catch. And then in Super Bowl IV he made the catch, just a little hitch pass, but he broke a tackle and scored. Those were the three biggest plays because I am talking about three teams. The Jets, Oakland, and Kansas City were great defenses that year.

Photograph copyright Associated Press

Chapter 27

Paul Hornung

> College:
> Notre Dame
>
> Career History:
> Green Bay Packers (1957-1962, 1964-1966)
>
> 1986 Inductee Pro Football Hall of Fame

College Choice
I actually wanted to go to Kentucky. I loved Bear Bryant. I got to know Babe Parilli, he was kind of like my idol in high school. I really hadn't thought about Notre Dame until they got into the picture. My mom, being a very strict Catholic gal, really wanted me to go to Notre Dame. Back in those days, athletes went to the college that their parents picked and that was the case for me.

I wasn't unhappy with it, for heaven's sakes. It's one of great places of all time. I had gotten to know Babe Parilli and Bear Bryant. Bear Bryant cleared the way with Adolph Rupp. He was the coach of basketball. I wanted to play basketball. I was All-State in basketball for two years. I don't know if Coach Rupp really liked the idea of giving me a chance to play with the basketball team, but I think Bear Bryant asked him to and he said okay. When I met with Coach Rupp and Coach Bryant, I kind of decided that I was going to go to Kentucky and try to play football and basketball. But my mom wanted me to go to Notre Dame, so case closed.

If you grew up in Kentucky, basketball is really the number one sport. It always has and always will be. We went to the state championships my senior year. I was All-State my junior and senior years, so I wanted to play. I did play a year at Notre Dame. I played when I was a sophomore. I made the team and was going to play my junior and senior years, but Terry Brennan, the coach at Notre Dame said, "You know Paul, it is too important for you to maintain your grades. If you play basketball and it is going to take you away from your studies, I would really appreciate it if you didn't." So I gave up basketball after my sophomore year at Notre Dame.

Positions Played at Notre Dame
I played quarterback my senior year all the way. I didn't play halfback. I think I was a real good defensive football player. I was a safety. I was second in the team with tackles, first in interceptions, and I played 60 minutes a game. Those were the days when you played 60 minutes, you played offence and defense of course. I enjoyed both parts of the game. We were two and eight for heaven's sakes. The only real bad point in my four years at Notre Dame was to have to remember that. Terry Brennan was the coach. They let him go a couple of years after that. I think that season dominated their thinking as far as Notre Dame was concerned about keeping Terry Brennan as coach.

Frank Leahy
The first day I was there, he called me up and said, "I want this guy to take you over to practice kicking." It was Johnny Lujack for heaven's sake. What a thrill. Then he had Lou Groza, helping with kicking drills, come in from Cleveland. I was ecstatic. To know that on my freshman team I was going to be tutored by Johnny Lujack was very, very important. He and I became great friends. He still shoots his age in golf. He is unbelievable. He is a hell of an athlete.

I enjoyed it. I enjoyed my four years at Notre Dame. I wouldn't take them back for anything in the world.

Nickname "The Golden Boy"
Tom Fitzgerald, a writer for the Courier, nicknamed me that. I had a real good day in the spring game against the seniors and veterans from the pro league who would come back. I was a sophomore quarterback. Ralph Guglielmi was to be the number one quarterback with Tom Carey, who is now president and owner of Hawthorne Race Track. I was a sophomore and Gugliemi and Carey were seniors.

Winning A Heisman Trophy On A Losing Team
You really gotta have some talent to do that. It has never been done since and probably never will be. I was in the top four or five when I was a junior. So I was kind of like the favorite. Jim Brown was right there with me. He got the highest votes behind me when I was a junior, so we were kind of the top two that they thought were going to beat John Brodie and Len Dawson. Tommy McDonald from Oklahoma was sensational in those days. Out of the top ten football players that came out of that year, when I was a senior, I think that all of them are in the College Hall of Fame and eight or nine of them are in the Pro Football Hall of Fame. It was a pretty good year.

The '57 College All-Star Game
He was a pain in the ass, Otto Graham. He didn't like me at all. He didn't like Notre Dame. Here was the Heisman Trophy winner from the University of Notre Dame going to Chicago. We had great quarterbacks on that team. We had Len Dawson and John Brodie. Otto Graham ran the offense. I told Curley Lambeau the Head Coach, "I will never forgive you. Here I am the number one pick of the draft, going to Green Bay and I don't start this game."

I was pissed off. He started Brodie and he didn't do anything. Then he put me in. He had Jim Brown, and he didn't even start Jim Brown. He didn't start Jim Brown and he is former Cleveland Brown. Well, he was really pissed, Brown was.

So when we got in in the second quarter, I called Brown's play six times and I threw him four flat passes and we scored a touchdown, the first one. Brown said, "God damn, you going to give me a break a little bit?" I said, "Nope. You are going to get it every time." So at halftime Brown said, "I'm suiting up. Come on lets go change clothes, I'm not playing for this guy."

So, it wasn't Curley. He relinquished all of his power to Otto on offense. He said, "I'm starting you and Brown after halftime." I said, "I don't know about Jimmy, but I'm not playing anymore, I'm finished. I'm afraid I'm going to get hurt Curley." I lied to him of course. He knew it. Jim Brown didn't play either. Brown refused to play. So we sat on the bench. Of course we got beat in the second half, not because of that, they were a better football team.

NFL Draft
I knew I was going to be a high pick. It didn't bother me. Shit like that doesn't bother me. If it happens it happens. I'm not looking forward to being number one in this or that. I have been very lucky in my career, being at Notre Dame, winning the Heisman and all of that, then being named the MVP of the NFL. I couldn't have had a better career in football for heaven's sake. I got to play under the greatest coaches. Vince Lombardi stood above the whole bunch, the best guy in the world for that. I look back on my career with great pride and I am happy.

Bonus Pick.
They had a bonus pick then, just like they do in basketball. You pick, you get the bonus pick then you are out of the pick. The rest of them are in. It runs through the whole league. There were two teams left in the bonus pick at that time. It was the Packers and the Chicago Cardinals.

That is where the franchise was. Back in the '50s, the St. Louis Cardinals were the Chicago Cardinals and they played at Comiskey Park. I wanted to be picked by the Cardinals because I had so many interests in Chicago, having gone to Notre Dame. I was going to go right into business with a couple of Chicago people, so I was kind of hoping to be picked by the Cardinals. Of course, I was picked by the Packers. I played in the All-Star game and went to Green Bay for 11 years.

I enjoyed my time with the Packers because of Lombardi. Lombardi changed it all around for Green Bay. He was one of a kind. I was a Green Bay Packer for those years.

First Packers Training Camp
It was fine. I didn't know where I was going to play. Curley Lambeau had set the stage for me, arriving at Notre Dame not having played that much in the All-Star game, the questions and all of the publicity. Of course, I didn't get along with Lisle Blackbourn. When I say I didn't get along, I didn't like him. I didn't think he was worth a shit, and he wasn't.

He played me halfback one week, but he wouldn't tell me until Saturday. We are going to use you at fullback this week. We are going to use you at halfback. What kind of a coach is that? I didn't even work out during the week at the position that he was hoping for me to play. So, I had a very poor rookie year as far as I was concerned. I didn't enjoy it whatsoever. I was establishing a pretty successful business in Louisville so I was actually thinking, to hell; I'm not going to put up with this guy all my life. I will just get out of it, and go on into real estate.

Then of course Vince Lombardi came and changed the whole thing. Not too many quarterbacks come out having made making All-American in college who make All Pro at another position in the NFL.

Vince Lombardi
Vince Lombardi took over. He was disciplined. He came in that first day and told us who was boss and we were going to do it his way or it was the highway. Either enjoy it or get your ass out. We all bought into it. After what we had been through the first two years when I was there, it was ridiculous. I was ready to hang it up. He talked me out of that and said that I could be a hell of a football player in his offense. He told me how he was going to use me throwing the football and running the football. He said, "I think you are athletic enough to block, so right now you are my halfback. If you don't screw it up, you are going to be successful in this league." And, I believed him.

Jerry Kramer
Name me one team that has 12 guys in the Hall of Fame. We should have 13. It's absolutely ridiculous that Jerry Kramer is not in. He was better than all of the guards in the league in his day.

He is not in the Hall of Fame, because of Alex Karras. See, Karras should have kept his mouth shut about killing Jerry Kramer because Karras was sensational. He was one of the greatest players I ever played against period! He was unblockable. Jerry Kramer couldn't have blocked him. He was the best guard in the league and he couldn't block him. You shouldn't hold that against one guy all his life. Some of these reporters, it just shows you that they don't know shit about football. To keep him out is ridiculous.

They kept me out. There was a guy in Baltimore who used to solicit votes against me. You wanna keep your mouth shut when you gotta vote. You do not need to talk to anyone else. It is kind of an unwritten law with the guys who vote on the Hall of Fame. This guy was adamantly against me. Now, there is somebody who has been adamantly against Jerry Kramer, and just because he had a hard time. He will tell you he had a hard time against Alex Karras. Alex Karras was the best tackle I played against.

There are other tackles that he would take care of who are in the Hall of Fame. It just pisses me off that Jerry is not in there. But, we have 12 guys off our team in the Hall of Fame. No team can even come close to that.

Dave Robinson
Dave Robinson was unblockable. Nobody blocked him. He also was on our team, a team that had many guys in the Hall of Fame. Writers get tired of voting for Packers. I can understand that to a point. But, believe me, I had to go up and block against him. I knew what kind of linebacker he was. I watched him practice and nobody was as good as he was.

Mike Ditka & Gale Sayers
I played against Mike Ditka. There was no better tight end that played the game than Ditka. If you played safety against Ditka, you were in trouble. You had to always know where he was, because when Gale Sayers would reverse his field, those poor safeties and defensive backs down there, they better know where Ditka was. It was kind of brutal. You would watch the film and all of a sudden Gale would switch gears and go somewhere else. Incidentally, when he first walked off Lambeau Field up in Green Bay, I grabbed a hold of him said, "Gale, you've got to work hard. Stay straight baby because you are going to be the best football player in this league, period." He did turn out to be that. I still think he is the best runner I have ever seen, period. Nobody is close.

Dick Butkus
I am going to tell you a great story about the Bears. This is a true story; a lot of people don't know this. When Vince Lombardi first took a look at Dick Butkus at his first game in the exhibition season, he said, "Oh he is

a little bit deep. Look at him. He is back there about six yards. He is six yards deep of middle linebacker. Now I know he makes the tackle here, but the guard misses him, the tackle misses him but yeah he kinda upset the whole … but we are going to be able to take care of this guy, he is too deep, and he doesn't get over there real quick. I know he got there and he stopped the play, but … "

We were leading the league in rushing at the time and I was running the ball about 12 or 13 times. Jimmy Taylor was running the ball about 25 times and we were gaining about 200 yards a game rushing. We played the Bears the first game against Butkus. I ran the ball about 13 times and I gained about 12 yards. Jimmy ran the ball 22 times and he normally was leading the league in rushing at the time, about 150 a game, Jimmy ran the ball 22 times and gained 44 yards. Butkus made like 24 tackles.

Chicago Bears Linebackers
Before that we had to face Bill George, so you know, we were kind of used to pretty good middle linebackers. George was one of the greatest linebackers of all time, who played before Dick. Anyway, Doug Atkins was unblockable. After Lombardi saw that, he said, "Look, he was sitting back there, you missed him, Forrest Gregg everybody misses this guy, he must be something special." And that is what Lombardi said after the first time and of course, what the hell, he did prove that he was special. It's ridiculous what he did. The film that I saw last week of Dick Butkus was the damndest film of a football player that I have seen as a linebacker. He killed people.

Rick Casares
Rick Casares was something. People do not realize what a tough son of a … I saved Ray Nitschke's life once because Nitschke broke Casares ankle. Casares never forgot. Casares said, "I'll get him." Casares dared Nitschke outside up in Appleton Wisconsin and of course Nitschke wouldn't go, he ain't going to go because Casares would have killed him.

I saw Casares hit a few people and it worried me to death. I thought he killed a guy on Rush Street one night. I mean, the guy made a remark about Casares girlfriend and Casares unloaded on him and his face disintegrated, just disintegrated. I jumped down and I pulled Casares off of the guy, or Casares would have killed him. Casares was unbelievable. Nobody was as tough as that, nobody fooled with him.

Photograph copyright Associated Press

Chapter 28

Jim Taylor

> College: Louisiana State
>
> Career History:
> Green Bay Packers (1958-1966)
> New Orleans Saints (1967)
>
> 1976 Inductee Pro Football Hall of Fame

College Choice
I got invited to go to other colleges. I made a couple of trips to other colleges to visit them. I came back home and said, "No. I'm going to stay in Baton Rouge, here at Louisiana State University." I wanted to be in my hometown in Baton Rouge.

LSU Teammates
Billy Cannon and Johnny Robinson who later played defensive back for the Kansas City Chiefs were teammates of mine. When Johnny went to Kansas City the AFL was just coming into existence. Billy Cannon was also courted by the AFL's Houston Oilers and Owner Bud Adams. Later on he went to Oakland Raiders where he ended up for most of his career. He was a running back at the college level and they moved him to tight end with the Raiders.

I was a middle linebacker in college. I probably had better games playing middle linebacker than I did running the ball. We just ran between the tackles and threw short passes.

Green Bay Packers
Green Bay's a special place and I stepped right in. When you're blocking big defensive ends or blitzing linebackers your job is to protect your quarterback. It's the job of moving up and maturing and becoming

a more polished player. In the NFL you just play one position, either the running back position or fullback. Paul Hornung, who had come to the Packers the year before, was the halfback and I was the fullback. Ron Kramer came from Michigan as a basketball player and tight end and stepped right in and played tight end.

I didn't play running back. I was on special teams and Scooter McLean came from the Detroit Lions as the head football coach. You got to see the whole, big picture. Then Vince Lombardi came the following year, in '59. When I got there in '58, we won one game. It was a learning experience where you had a very weak team and lots of older players. Then, we got it right. The next year we got Willie Davis and we got some others that we traded for. Henry Jordan was picked up by the Packers. In the first year we had one victory. My first year, I only played in games in California. We left Detroit after we played our Thanksgiving Day game and went on to California to play L.A. and San Francisco. I think they realized the coach was going to be gone so I was put in to be the running back in both those games. We didn't win but I gained over a hundred and some odd yards in both games but we lost them. I had the feeling I think I can play professional football as a running back.

I wasn't involved in the social life in Green Bay. I came to the Green Bay Packers to play football in that little town. I'm a pretty straight shooter. I really dedicated myself to training and fitness and I said I'm going to be the best physical conditioned player on this football team because I knew I was going to get the ball twenty-five, twenty-eight times game in and game out. I knew that my fitness level had to be at its peak.

Vince Lombardi
Vince Lombardi came to Green Bay and he knew what he wanted to do, how he wanted to coach his team, and how he wanted to lead them. We had some decent talent because we got some good draft picks in the first year or two. We were in the championship in 1960. It was his second year, I think. We were 7-5 his first year. We were 1-10-1 was my rookie year and the second year were 7-5. The next year we were playing the Philadelphia Eagles in Franklin Field for the championship of the National Football League. It was a pretty swift and short turnaround.

It's a big step up in class knowing that you moved up towards the top to compete against solid football teams. Now, you have to leave the outhouse and try to move closer to the penthouse.

It was amazing. Lombardi was an assistant coach at the high school level and then at Army. After that, he went on to the New York Giants. He knew what he wanted to do with his experience working with different coaches and teams. When he got to Green Bay, he said this is the formula, and this is the format for playing championship football. He started to put together personnel for all the positions. Now, we've got 11 players in the Pro Football Hall of Fame. You could see the tradition and the history of the Green Bay Packers being established after Lombardi arrived. He had a great team and a great concept of teamwork on both sides of the ball. He just wouldn't let anyone be bigger than the team. Everyone was expected to play, do his job, and be a very tough and good football player.

<u>Winning NFL Rushing Title in 1962 The Only Year Jim Brown Didn't Win it During His Career</u>
I won the rushing title in 1962, with outstanding blocking and outstanding coaching, and me making my contribution with the football.

Paul Hornung was there but I think he was injured, so we had Elijah Pitts and Tom Moore filling in for Paul. The offensive line was very explosive. I was able to read our offensive linemen's blocking and then maximize the yardage on a play. I just got acclimated. It's a matter of making really quick decisions and having split vision to be able to see the blocking and things. I was quick, had good balance, and tried to stay low and do things as an instinctive type of a runner.

We knew we had some good backups with Tom Moore and Elijah Pitts. We might have had some other players and running backs who we could plug in when we had injuries to our first teamers.

I was so fortunate and lucky I didn't miss too many games. I didn't have too many injuries in my whole career. All my joints now, my ankles, my knees, my hips, my shoulders, and all are functional. I didn't have any procedures or surgeries in my 10 years at the professional level.

Ray Nitschke
Ray Nitschke was a great player and very aggressive player. He just led our defense. They were so strong. People haven't given the Packer defense all the credit that they deserve. People talk about Bart Starr, the receivers, Paul Hornung, and myself but the defense had outstanding players. They were just solid because game in and game out, they would just get the job done and kept teams from scoring. They just shut them down.

After First Championship Did The Packers Players Think It Was The Start Of A Dynasty?
A dynasty? I don't think so. I don't know that. We really wanted to follow Lombardi. We needed and wanted leadership. We were just starving for leadership. The Hornung team, I think, we went 1-10-1, the worst in Packer history. It was just a complete turnaround because the personnel were there. It's just a matter of getting the players to work together and maximize their ability. With the talent we had and the players looking to Vince Lombardi for leadership and motivation it all come together. The 12-2 or the 11-3 seasons were pretty good seasons with young players with Lombardi only being with the team for two or three years. It started from the grassroots and it started to build and it went real fast because the talent was there and the leadership was there and the productivity and the results were evident.

Max McGee
Max McGee was a different type of player and he was phenomenal. He was a good competitor. I remember seeing him play at Tulane in his college days. He was a running back at that level at that time and moved to the wide out in the NFL.

Max McGee's nickname was Paper Head. He wouldn't really stick his head in there to make a whole lot of blocks. He was a good competitor with great hands and a good leader on our team because of his humor.

Green Bay Packers Attitude
Back in those days, the egos and all about me attitude did not exist. Our football team was not individually hungry to be on television on in the newspaper. They just wanted to be team players and do their job. That is my attitude, sitting here in my house today. I wanted to play football and

be the best football player. I didn't worry about the money or about the publicity or whether I'd get All-Pro or this or that. That wasn't the mentality of our football team or myself. Today's players have a little different perceptive and have a little different attitude than our football team.

Forrest Gregg, Fuzzy Thurston, Jim Ringo, Willie Wood, Herb Adderley, and Willie Wood, these people came to be orientated with the team concept. It's just so hard for anybody in today's generation to understand that. You can tell today's generation over and over and over and it just doesn't resonate, it doesn't penetrate to their perceptive. You see where I'm coming from.

That and that the game itself on the field is no different. They still play with four to five second intervals on either side of the ball. Once the quarterback calls the play and snaps the ball, it's thousand-one, thousand-two, thousand-three, thousand-four, play's over with. You have a team actually playing only 12 to 13 minutes out of a three hour game. This is what the average fan cannot possibly comprehend and this is the way football is played. That is some of Lombardi's inspiration and the leadership that he instilled in our Packer football team that this is the way it's played, with explosion, whether it's a running play, a passing play, it does not matter. Once the play's over with, you go off the field.

Nobody wants to talk about what the basis of the game is. The game of football is explosion and doing your job and blocking, tackling, and moving those chains. Running and picking up whatever yards are needed to move the chains. The average fan cannot possibly understand or comprehend what I'm saying.

Vince Lombardi's Speech Prior To Super Bowl I
It was to go back and do what we did all week. We worked on first down and we worked on explosion. We worked on getting ourselves mentally tough to play the game against the opponent. We were looking at films all week of the opponent evaluating and looking at their players. They're going to block either on the run or pass.

Once the game is over on Monday morning you start to look at where you broke down and what it cost you and if you lost, it's amplified. With winning and exploding, by going 12-2 and 13-1 you're not as concerned but you still have to go back home and recoup and work on your weak points and your breakdowns. Lombardi tried to get you to be perfect, which is impossible. He required you to block 100% on the pass and a 100% on the run.

It's just that you're there to do your job and you love the competition. That is the point. Just forget about the media and all this talk and all this crap. Let's put the ball on the field. This is the only thing I had in my head. Let me hit these guys. Give me the ball. See? Now, you see, you're excited about exploding and doing your job for the fans to enjoy you making field goals, touchdowns and winning. That's the ultimate thing. We have our 11 players on offense and 11 on defense. Here again, fans cannot understand that either. You can write, you can talk, and I could preach this over and over and over and the fans would not understand it.

New Orleans Saints
I came home to New Orleans, Louisiana, and joined their expansion team and that was it. I made my choice to play with that team and at the end of that one season, I said I will go into scouting and radio and continue to fulfill my contractual agreements. I wasn't disturbed that this could possibly happen after one year of playing. There wasn't anybody in the dark. There wasn't any living in denial that my career was coming to an end. I was willing to accept it and move on.

Induction Pro Football Hall of Fame
It seriously a great feeling to be inducted into the Pro Football Hall of Fame and be recognized by your peers. It's just a wonderful feeling and your just cherishing the moment. You just kind move on. It's like scoring a touchdown or having the winning catch. It's just a real gratifying, self-satisfying feeling that you achieved or competed. The ultimate is to do the best job you can do and being inducted is giving you that recognition. Then, you move on. I mean, that's it. Put it behind you and then continue to climb more mountains.

Green Bay Packer Jim Taylor is brought down by Detroit Lion Dick Lane. Photograph copyright Associated Press

Chapter 29

Jim Brown

> College:
> Syracuse
>
> Career History:
> Cleveland Browns (1957–1965)
>
> 1971 Inductee Pro Football Hall of Fame

<u>College Choice</u>
I had a mentor, Judge Kenny Molloy from Manhasset. He also went to Syracuse. He took an interest in all of the kids out in Manhasset. He helped a lot of us tremendously. He wanted me to go to his alma mater and made arrangements for the people in the city to pay my way in and send me there on trial. It was a fiasco in the beginning, but it finally worked out. It wasn't because of him that it was a fiasco. I don't think Syracuse wanted me at that time, but since he wanted me to go there they followed through. I really had to prove myself about five times. Now I'm a real good alumnus of Syracuse.

I just wasn't one of the choices of at least some of the coaches there. Head Coach Ben Schwartzwalder was a different kind of guy. They had another African American there by the name of Avatus Stone. He was a quarterback, but he left them and went to Canada and played football. I think he had a lot of resentment. We had something in common being of the same color. I didn't know the guy. They had problems with having African American players there that were independent individuals. I ended up being the only African American player on the team.

I love ball sports and I tried to play as many as I could. At Syracuse, football and lacrosse were my two main sports. Lacrosse was a game I loved because the coach was a great coach and his son and I were really good friends. We're friends today. We went undefeated in our senior year, which was really good. It's a great game that has a Native American background. It was created by the Native Americans and used to be Canada's national sport. A lot of people never knew that. Now I think it's the fastest growing sport in this country.

Why I Chose to Play Professional Football
I had a better shot at being a professional football player than any other sport. I took advantage of it. I had nine years as a member of the Cleveland Browns that were very successful and very happy years. I never really played for money. I never did anything for money only. As I've said, I'm an all-around athlete because I love pretty much all sports. I was also a decathlete. When I was a senior in high school I finished 5th in the nation, which I was very proud of because I had no coaching.

Paul Brown
Paul was a very creative individual. He was a visionary. He was a great pioneer for professional football. He created certain things like the playbook and the facemask. He was an individual that was sometimes misunderstood, but I liked playing under him because he was a very strict disciplinarian. Everybody was afraid of him so the team really stuck together and concentrated on playing football, which was what I really liked.

Paul relied on me a lot and I loved it. I wanted the ball and I got it enough to be a very successful running back.

On Being Called Greatest Football Player Ever
I'm going to be real honest with you. I don't live my life based on trophies, awards, or opinions. I respect a lot of opinions. I have my own. When your teammates or opposing players feel that you are a great competitor, that's a good compliment. That's a solid compliment because they usually won't tell anything or say anything that they don't believe. I can take that, accept that compliment to a certain degree but I usually know what I can do, what I can't do. I really know how I performed. I'm my greatest critic. I don't think anyone has ever heard me say that I'm the best at anything, because I think that we shouldn't try to judge ourselves. There are too many variables in a team sport. If it

was boxing or something like that it would be different, but in team sports you depend upon each other. Lebron James has proven himself to be a great team player and I love him for it because people overlook the greatness of a team player. Magic Johnson, Larry Bird, and Bill Russell, are the types of individuals that I like because they understood team sports and how important the last guy on your team is, because he might be the difference in winning and losing.

1964 Browns Team

We had a good team and everybody participated in that '64 game. We beat the Baltimore Colts and they were like a Hall of Fame team. They had many Hall of Famers on the team. The great Johnny Unitas was the quarterback, Raymond Berry was there, John Mackey was there, and "Big Daddy" Lipscomb was there. It was an unbelievable team and we beat them twice. I think they lost by three touchdowns and we had individuals that did their jobs tremendously and we were able to shut them out. Once again the offense got all the credit but the defense didn't allow them to score a point. That just goes to show you that sometimes the media or public opinion isn't always what we see as players. We have a great appreciation for the contribution of others that a lot of times, the general public doesn't even see.

Sam Huff

Sam Huff made a lot of tackles. Sam was a great middle linebacker for the Giants, and he was very smart. Sam was a good friend of mine, a good advocate for professional football, and played on some really great Giant teams. He was a leader on those teams and I always had great respect for him and great respect for his abilities.

Playing Defense

I did play defense in college. I was a decent safety in college. All throughout my athletic career I played defense but as a pro we didn't. We played one way and that was good enough for me because in professional football you have to really concentrate and it was difficult to play both positions.

Speed

I was fast and my speed was combined with my balance, strength, and power. I had a combination of things that all worked together. You might be the fastest guy in the world but if you don't use it properly, it doesn't really materialize into anything. I was fast enough. I never got beat in a 40. I always worked on my starts as a high school football player because my coach wanted me to. It gave me an advantage because I could get out of the blocks real quick. It always helps in professional football if you can really accelerate quickly. It's a great asset to have.

Larry Wilson
Larry Wilson's number was 8. Now how would I remember a guy's number? When I first came in contact with him, he tackled me and I didn't know where he came from. I looked down, and the number 8 was on his jersey. I went back and asked my teammates, who wore number 8. He put a hell of a tackle on me because that guy was too small to stop me but he did. He caught me around the ankles and I said, "You know, we're going to have to watch out for him." Then two plays later he did the same thing. I said, "We are really going to have to watch out for him because he can really play. I think he was one of my favorites because he was a smaller guy but very good at tackling big guys like me, getting low, wrapping our ankles up. When your ankles are wrapped up, you can't employ too much power. I've always had a lot of respect for Larry.

Retiring at Height of Career
Leaving football was not hard for me at all because I am a well-rounded person. I'm a college graduate. I'm an activist. I've been an activist all of my life. I have an organization now called Amer-I-Can. We work in schools across the country. We work with violence across the country. I got Earth, Wind, & Fire their first record contract. I've done many, many things in my life. I've been an entrepreneur in many ways and I try to be as much of a humanitarian as I can be. I have a very well-rounded life.

I took an interest in doing other things rather than just being an athlete. To me it was the wise thing to do. I knew that my legacy would be based on the fact that I had left at age 29. We won the championship in 1964. I was MVP of the league in 1965. The legacy stands very tall because I did leave at the height of my career.

People stay too long. There's no reason to stay that long. It's only a part of your life. You should not put too much importance on it. Your education is going to ultimately prove to be the best thing you can acquire. If you do not understand economic development then you're going to have a problem. I think of all the money that the players make today. After three years most of them declare bankruptcy, which is a shame.

Gale Sayers
Gale Sayers is a dear friend of mine. He is a wonderful human being and a very smart young man. I love him. I have nothing but respect for him. You have to manage your money especially if you make a lot because the more you make, the more trouble you can get into. The one thing that will always be a major problem is taxes. In your financial planning you have to take taxes into consideration very strongly. If it's not in your plan properly, it can back fire on you later. Once you're in trouble with the IRS, you're really in trouble.

Regardless how much money you make, you have to really manage it properly. You must consider your taxes, and any kind of deferred payments have to be allowable. You have to be very careful with your investments. Very few players manage their money correctly. Very few agents can really tell players the truth because players will fire the agent if he is not just talking about making more money. In order to really be successful you have got to live off an allowance. Each year you have to decide what it is that you can live off of, pay the proper taxes, and have the balance that you need. When people make a lot of money they think they can just spend a lot of it.

Decision to Become an Actor
It was an opportunity that knocked on my door. I was offered a part in a movie because I was a football player and had some notoriety. After I did that part, I decided to get an agent and he got me a part in "The Dirty Dozen", which was a tremendous hit. I got good reviews. It gave me the chance to have a high profile profession that paid me a lot of money? I tried it. I had an opportunity to break down a few doors, break down some taboos and I had a lovely acting career.

The movie 100 Rifles was quite an experience because it was the first time that an African American male had a major love scene with a Caucasian female. There was a lot made of Raquel Welch and I doing it at the time. It was like breaking down doors. I enjoyed it because I felt, not only was I making money, I had a chance to do something different. I felt I could probably open up opportunities for people that deserved opportunities. I looked at it that way and did some meaningful films.

My favorite actor was Al Pacino. Al Pacino is a great actor, a Hall of Fame actor, and a great guy. I had a couple of real scenes with him. Yes, I had the pleasure of working with him on some meaningful scenes. With him being such a nice guy, it was just a great experience.

Fred Williamson
I appreciated Fred Williamson's intelligence. Fred was a producer and a director and he did a lot of small films, which I acted in with him. I have admiration for his ability to understand the business and cut a niche out in the business for himself. As far as competition, I only compete with myself. I never got into competing with other people. This whole "best" thing, I think is it's a weakness to go around talking about you are the best at something. Your performance speaks for itself, your actions speak for themselves and if you're confident with yourself you don't have to really get into, 'Who is the best?'

Photograph copyright Associated Press